A RUNNER'S HEART
CHUCK CORNELIUS

Illustrations by
AMY I. HARRIS

Chuck Cornelius
Route 1, Box 336 - AA
Vincent, Ohio 45784
(740) 678-2310

Printed in the United States of America
by
Richardson Printing Corporation
Marietta, Ohio

Endorsements

Chuck writes from the heart, and his expressive style captures the essence and soul of running. His book is valuable to all runners who have a passion for our sport. *DELMIR DOS SANTOS (BRAZIL)*

I am sure you will find friends and fans who will love to read this book. Fans who like to read poetry and stories instead of results, times, facts, and running stats. *EDDY HELLEBUYCK (BELGIUM)*

Chuck is one of the more unique people I've met in my roadracing travels. He's put lots of hard work into this book, and it's as unique as he is. *KELLIE CATHEY ARCHULETTA (NEVADA)*

I found this collection of stories and poems very interesting. It offers the insight of a mid-pack runner relating the wonders of running that all runners feel. *DAN HELD (WISCONSIN)*

This is a wonderful book! I appreciate Chuck's honesty in "First Marathon." The book brings me a flood of precious running memories. *KITTY CONSOLO (OHIO)*

I really like Chuck's book best because it makes me think – of noble thoughts, the simple gifts of Nature, and the joy and peace I feel whenever I run. *JENNIFER MARTIN (PENNSYLVANIA)*

I have read Chuck's book twice, and I feel it is great. Keep it up! *MONIQUE ECKER (NEW MEXICO)*

Chuck's poetry takes a runner through every "gear." In his stories of races the runners really come alive as persons. The short story "The End of the Road" is a special one. *DARRELL GENERAL (MARYLAND)*

In his poetry Chuck is paying attention to life. His thoughts reflect depth, insight, and spirituality. I reflected on his poetry like daily prayer. His expression captures the moments of road running life. *DOUG KURTIS (MICHIGAN)*

For my parents

Charles "Corky" and Margaret June Cornelius, who taught me values by their example, to celebrate the goodness of life, to keep on going when things are tough, and to tie my running shoes carefully!

Contents

ILLUSTRATIONS

———•◦|◦•———

About the Author

Chuck Cornelius grew up in the hills of South Charleston, West Virginia. He remembers being the second fastest in his class in quarter-mile races in gym class in junior high. He first took up running in 1971 unofficially in a 20-Mile Walk for Mankind in Milford, Michigan, when he became bored after a mile or two of walking. He repeated this "victory" in 1972 although three high school runners caught him at 15 miles. He bought them treats at the local Dairy Queen in return for their promise not to pass the "old guy."

He coached high school cross country in Ohio, beginning in 1980, and his young Warren Warriors (mostly freshmen and sophomores) were conference champions in 1981. Inspired and excited about running, he increased his training and began to enter more races. He also directed a few local distance runs and enjoyed giving away unusual random prizes.

In 1985 Chuck completed his first marathon at Ohio's oldest, the Athens Marathon. On a hot, humid day 40 per cent of the field dropped out. Chuck was way back (99th place) but was happy to finish. Just four weeks later he knocked nearly 40 minutes off his time at the Revco Marathon in Cleveland. Six days later he learned a little something about pain as he tackled the monstrous hills of Wheeling, West Virginia, in the Big Boy Classic 20K.

He competes in several states and sometimes invents a lively costume to give a race something special. He writes regularly for the *Runner's Gazette* in Lewisburg, Pennsylvania, and is a member of the River City Runners Club in Parkersburg, West Virginia. He's always ready to try a new race. Chuck urges you to keep on running - and keep the fun in it, too!

About the Illustrator

Amy I. Harris has been drawing since she was only two years of age. Her mother considered her 'little stick people' to be "impressive." She earned a Bachelor's degree in Illustration at Ohio University in Athens, Ohio. *A Runner's Heart* is her first published piece. Says Amy, "I like to create a mood in my illustrations, to express what I am seeing to my audience." Amy makes her home in Belpre, Ohio, with her husband Paul, who is also a runner, and their son Ian.

Foreword by Bill Rodgers

I enjoyed reading *A Runner's Heart*. It's quite a mixture of poetry, journal record keeping, and philosophy on what running means to Chuck Cornelius, whom I've known for seven or eight years. This book is indeed from the heart every bit of the way.

Chuck pulls no punches in his love affair for running – one I relate to – and I think you will, too. He has a sharp eye for the things that count in running, the connection to the trees, plants, and animals he sees on his runs – and it is this connection that too many people have lost in our country. If you don't spend some time moving (and I don't mean in a car) and some time with Mother Nature, I believe you are on the deficit side of life. I can tell from *A Runner's Heart* that Chuck believes this, too. Chuck has some fascinating stories to tell about some of his races, and they often have a twist to them that leaves you saying, "You're right, Chuck!"

When I first met Chuck, I knew he had a unique point of view about his running; now I know why. Chuck is an ace – I can't believe you'll read this book and disagree with me.

Preface

Running to me epitomizes the very best in life. I actually began running as a lifestyle and hobby in midstream, my late thirties – past my prime, you might say. But running since my first race in 1978 on a hilly course in Marietta, Ohio, has been a constant companion and something that has led me to express a kaleidoscope of thoughts and emotions that it has generated.

I feel it is time to share these magical moments with you. May you forever be inspired and richly satisfied every time you lace up your running shoes. The joys I have known through running have sustained me through good times and bad. It is my hope that many of these writings will mean something special to you. All of us are privileged to be runners, a noble and honest calling.

———•◦•◦•———

Acknowledgments

Writing this book has been a joyful labor. With the generous encouragement of many I have been able to share the depth of my love for running.

Among those whom I'd like to thank for their help are: Art McCafferty, who introduced me to long-distance running; Freddi and Harry Carlip, whose *Runner's Gazette* provided me the opportunity to sharpen my writing skills; the boys of Warren Local High School, who let me tag along as coach to win the crown as well as to have innumerable good times together; the best runners of the USA and world, who say they can see themselves and their feelings in my work; the average, middle, and back-of-the-pack runners, whose hopes and spirit I represent; beginners, who continue to inspire me with their zest for our sport; champions I have known, especially Bill Rodgers, John Campbell, Steve Spence, and Priscilla Welch, who have set high standards for performance and sportsmanship; Sam Guy, M.D., (now a runner himself) who has helped me recover from bouts with depression; my wife Martha, who has traveled with me to races all over the country and has listened patiently to most of the poems, stories, and essays found herein, transferring to me her unbridled strength to keep on trying for publication; special runners who are friends forever – Carl Hatfield, Jamie Comer, Dr. Kitty Consolo, Jeanne Dorton, Norma Phillips, and Bob Brotherton; the immortal spirits of Steve Prefontaine, Dr. George Sheehan, and Fred Lebow (he passed me one memorable day in April at mile seven of the Nike Cherry Blossom Run); Amy I. Harris, illustrator, whose pictures have interpreted my themes with beauty, taking them to a new dimension. To everyone else I have met along the way, you, too, are a part of this book and of this runner's heart.

———•◦•◦•———

The Warmup

The old order changeth, yielding place to new
and God fulfills himself in many ways,
lest one good custom should corrupt the world.

Alfred, Lord Tennyson

Today

Today is the only day I have. Yesterday is gone, and tomorrow but a dream. I rejoice in the company of my students. My hope is that I will have a good run today after school and feel the warm October sun bring out a generous sweat on this body, yearning for the simplicity of play, the honesty of running, and cold refreshments afterwards as a toast to friendship and being alive. To life!

You are with me on the peaks

They shall mount up with wings as eagles.

Isaiah 40:31

Because

Because the shoes feel so right on my feet
   And the sun, wind, and clouds await me every day
Because the good thoughts stream down in proliferation
   And toots and waves bring a smile to my face.

Because the woods and waters comfort me
   And the shorts highlight muscular legs
The bandanna reflects my free-spirit stance on life
   As I'm facing traffic, chasing a dream.

Because it's a far better friend than many
   Its lessons are honest, enduring, and humbling
I pulsate, I radiate joy
   Because life's a two-way street, I'm out there.

An Eagle's Wings

"Whooo! Whooooo!" the wintry air speaks to me
    A lone runner on austere paths
Here not by chance but by design
    I chart the course in the new-fallen snow
So that others may follow
    But only if they choose.

How did it start?
    "Why's that guy out there in this
kind of weather, Harry?" she asks
    As they pass swiftly by in automobilian comfort
And laziness,
    Not understanding one iota.

As I near the crest of Route 98,
    Three deer approach the two lanes
Two vault on across the chasm
    Softly I coax the third to follow suit
"Go ahead, fella, it's still safe; you can make it!"
    He does.

Warmed by the ascent
    I, too, feel like my brother and sister deer
As I coast downward with little strain
    The sweat forming icicles
On face, toboggan, and mitten tips
    This is honest work and play.

This regimen of honest sweat
    Teaches more than words can say
Starting out for six miles or more
    Is, in part, a matter of faith
Like planting a tree
    Or having a child.

A runner, a happy wanderer I
    Explorer, Thoreau, Whitman, Johnny Appleseed,
All wrapped up in one
    Proud to be one of the world's doers
A low pulse rate, a growing patience
    To survive, cope with, ignore life's farces.

So it all comes back to love
    This running thing, this little hobby
That takes me to races hither and yon,
    Also brings me back to my senses
I feel the warm shower after the run
    God is good; thankful for everything, I cherish this moment.

Melody

Twenty-five degrees, four miles, three hills
    The throttle cut back, just resting my gills
When over the bridge and stretched out 'cross the lake
    Flashed a beautiful sight, oh, make no mistake.

The quick western wind churned the lake into riffles
    And had I been a frog, well, 'twould have given me sniffles
As the sun bore down right out of the south
    Painted truth so majestic and a smile on my mouth.

In my mind's eye I gleaned that the wave swept on east
    And that I was privileged to witness the feast
And in this wide world where we play no small parts
    I've just been granted the "Doctor of Arts."

Well, if I'm Ph. D., pile it higher and steeper
    Give me uphills and downhills, may I see beauties deeper
Help me love thy creation and be kind to all creatures
    And keep spirit aflame to enjoy simple features.

For it's not great riches make us grin ear to ear
    But the friends, small things, love that we share while we're here
Keep watching for riffles, the water, and wind
    Your garden of memories will bloom 'til the end.

———◆•◈•◆———

The Champion

The warmup now is over
I toe the starting line
It seems to be a special day
I'm ready, feeling fine.

Occasions come once in a while
When training peaks together
When you explode to mile one
However tough the weather.

You hold that pace at mile three
And to the lead you're close
A certain spring is in your step
A SPIRIT "overdose."

Race ebbs and flows, you're hanging tough
Your strategy is working
You build and play with speed once more
Your duties never shirking.

The finish line looms up ahead
You win, your face agleam
But then you're startled by a "pop!"
For it was just a dream.

A Runner's Prayer

O Runner of Runners, I praise thee
I am thankful for every day
That I am able to send my body in motion
Cutting a brief swath in eternity.

Brother wind, refreshing me always
Not always helping, but keeping me company
Making me alert, intrepid, resilient
Teaching me patience, composure, grace.

Sunshine, in my face, you're always welcome
You energize me, inspire and heighten my performance
In the midst of your majesty I don't ask questions
I just glide onward on my quest, chasing a dream.

Elemental, primeval, primitive, necessary
I complete the course and feel a glow
Unable to fathom most of this whirling universe
A sense of calm washes my soul.

This passion, I know, beats in your heart, too
I am the spirit of running, festive and free
Next time you hit the trail, road, or track
Be of good cheer, for I am with you always.

The Vow

I slowly scale Olympus mount
    Drink nectar from the flowing fount
Whate'er I do, where'er I roam
    This fertile soil will be my home.

Here wisdom's race I do begin
    I face the world with impish grin
When Fate rains down its sharpest dart
    I rise again with grateful heart.

The torch is passed to you and me
    For a short time we honor thee
Our words and deeds will long proclaim
    The sacred honor of thy name.

We give the best we have to give
    And to the hilt we pledge to live
And when we've reached a higher place
    We'll loudly sing "Amazing Grace."

Caretakers All

We are here but little time
    Poets like me will make their rhyme
The world's a spinning, devious orb
    And this the message to absorb.

That we are part of the glorious plan
    To recognize the good in man
To love our neighbors as ourselves
    And dust the trophies on our shelves.

Because we're here to get along
    To run, to dance, to sing our song
Helping defuse hot conflicts raging
    And running, gosh, combats our aging.

We take each day and with it run
    And radiate love, toil, and fun
Whate'er we do we do it well
    Our time is now to catch the spell!

What Is It?

Propulsion, pure and simple
Survival and pursuit, bred into us over the centuries
A means to an end
A goal to set, a race to finish.

Poetry in motion
A rhythm of breathing, arms, and legs
Delicate dancing on angels' wings
Incessant pounding up mountain peaks.

Escape, a look inward, a rebirth each new run
Release, the crowd's roar, the clean scent of body
Friendship, fellowship, Believers eating and laughing together
Aglow and vibrant, eternal children at play.

It is beyond words.

———◆•✦•◆———

Hot August Dreams

Morning's light beckons me,
"Come outside and play!"
I slip on shorts, shirt, and shoes
And calmly seize the day.

I head out north as usual
The pace is sure and slow
The aim to build endurance
However far I go.

A patch of fog envelopes me
As I crest the second hill
Its splendid beauty lifts my heart
I know it always will.

At run's end I hike downhill
Far out from the bridge a blue heron is
Startled by my passing
And calls, "Alarm! You might do harm!"
As she flies away into the foggy finger of yon lake.

Still don't know if I'll stay the course
Two grueling, long August races set to fly
But, sweaty body, honorable toil
I'll love thee, running, 'til I die.

64 Hours * (Next Stop: Wheeling)

* May be sung to the tune "26 Miles." If you know this one, you're an ex-teenager from the fabulous fifties and still "smoking" the racing circuit like a man or woman 20 years younger!

64 hours 'til the starter's gun
Wheeling's hills are lots of fun
To prepare, I'm soaking in the sun
Romance, romance, romance, romance.

Runners all around us everywhere
Tropical heat and humid air
Wear a costume? I wouldn't dare!
Romance, romance, a romance.

An exotic city loaded with racing fans
Challenging right from its birth
Hospitality coming your way
Surpasses any on this planet Earth.

20 kilometers for a national champ
And the medical tent will massage my cramps
Guess it's time to acknowledge, "Yup, I'm a gramp,"
Romance, romance, a romance.

Part II

(No tune for this unless you write one)

The sun is penetrating
It has mellowed me out
And my friendly partner, running,
Reigns tops with no doubt.

The world grows hot and bothered
With one issue or the other
And to lighten the load 'long life's twisting road
Why, running's as caring as Mother.
Out there on my loops
Why, it all comes together –

Contentment, Thankfulness, Compassion, Humility –
Free for the asking in all kinds of weather.

More summer days we need, just like these
But, oh my gosh, I've gotta sneeze.

Honeysuckle Heaven

Two days ago on a training run
I thought I'd take it just for fun
Little did I know that 'round the bend
There'd be perfume without end.

I turned left on 805
Avoiding the traffic rush, no jive!
Just after the bridge, watched ducklings scurry for home,
Up wafted the fragrance, bidding me roam.

So potent it was I started to chuckle
Yes, you guessed it, honeysuckle
Many more times on that rare, rare day
Nature's nectar floated my way.

The pleasant meandering in due course ended
And I turned from my run to a fence to be mended
When that same sweet aroma flooded my senses
Why, 'twas in full flower on one of my fences.

So maybe this memory will suffice
To help you recall one equally nice
And to top it off, I swallowed deeply the honeysuckle juice
Blame it on the nectar if this verse seems loose!

Barechested, One More Time

October twenty-five broke crisp and cool
I took care of business, and it turned into a jewel
After painting the new sign and hogging the brush
Three hours past lunch I suited up with a rush.

The first mile up was done purposely slow
But into sleek rhythm my body did grow
Now gently eased after yesterday's dances
The muscles' retreats now became bold advances.

Columbus, Columbus, I do love you so
Your 5K and 1OK glide past with the flow
And working the marathon, conditions the best
Encouraging the weary made this lad seek rest.

Instead 0-15-hundred saw us at the party
Refreshments abounded, the D.J. was hearty
My shirt sopping wet as I came back for more
Locomotion to polka, feet crisscrossed the floor.

Yes, yes, I've decided, the 1OK next year
The tangential turns will know I've been here
November 12-13 now marked on the wall
Will pay perfect tribute to a brisk day in fall.

Now back to the workout, I floated, I flit
And ever so quickly the "wire" I did hit
A walk-trot for home as I savored the day
A barechested boy, ruddy cheeks, at play.

Catch the Wave!

Late May, what a day!
North wind up, how full my cup!
This is the day for my last training run
Easy and slow, just savor the fun.

While kneeling down by gardenside
I am overwhelmed with pride
The sun beams through my apple tree
Indeed the best in life is free.

The whirling world goes speeding by
So little time before I die
So milk out every ounce of joy
And spread your wings, my precious boy.

I'll start with what I know the best
And plant the seed, you do the rest
For if you make the dream your own
You'll grow, your troubles will have flown.

Just be the best that you can be
Take on a challenge, plant a tree
Be a true friend and nourish, care
You can find goodness anywhere.

So catch your wave and chart your course
Pray for strength and patient force
Endurance for the winding way
As songs and laughter crown your day.

Real Value

I sit alone in midst of yard
But even here I'm on my guard
For two days ago on one of riding lawnmower's passes
Our apple tree bent down and ate my sunglasses.

Fortunately I had a spare
And you can bet I'll not lose them there
"Old apple tree, I love ya still
Bet you can't run up Heartbreak Hill!"

June wind drives hard out of the south
If I don't feel toasty, well, hush my mouth
The harried world goes whizzing by
Near you, o garden, just let me lie.

Traveling birds are feeding young
I marvel at the deeds they've done
They sing their songs, I'm glad they're here
To urge me on, keep soul in gear.

It's easy to be tossed about
By worldly claims and tales tall
But we'll not sit around and pout
When I'm in my garden, I have it all.

I won't prolong the agony
You've guessed the punchline true
You know where this is going
The rest is up to you.

And as for me 'ere sunset
Give me my trusty bowl
I'll fill it deep with cherries ripe
Make runners' pie my goal.

Six days ago granddaughters two
Megan and Lauren around me flew
Planted green beans and ran full out
Reminded me what life's about.

It's comforting to keep in hand
That we're part of a master plan
So live with gusto, jump for joy
To thyself be true, dear girl or boy.

Delicious

November the third?!
And who would believe it,
Southerly breezes adorn a day that feels
A perfect seventy-two.

Election Day - they gave us the day off from work
Naturally I elected to go running
Wind in my face, wind at my side
What did it matter, I was out there.

Out where I belong
An integral part of the hills and trails
Feeling as one now with the universe
After my run refreshed my soul.

"Good job, you're doing great!" I greeted
Dozens of other runners and walkers
Who dotted the park
As birds magnificently sang springtime songs.

Say, the Parkersburg Race for Safety was a hoot
And this costumed warrior had a ball
And would you believe Waynesburg's race director
Jeff Hughes wants nattily attired "dudes and babes"
At his fastest 5K in America November 21?

Whoa, sport,
This summer air is making me wax
Non-poetic.
Let me return to the writer's groove
If I can.

This day is like a bonus, grab it while we may
It will fend off pain and sorrow
Which winter brings our way
And if I paint the picture well
And share it thus with you
It may bring light within your heart
When daylight hours are few.

The only sounds I now can hear
Are oak leaves rustling loudly,
The only sight my eyes can see
Red maples blazing proudly
The gust picks up, the glow remains
Our day is on the wane
Delicious memories linger on
Sustain us 'til we meet again.

Friends in Autumn's Glory

This morning cirrus and stratus clouds
Roll gracefully southeast
As runners gather in Morgantown
For this treat, this feast.

I view a married couple
Two sugar maple trees
Arrayed in all their glory
Glistening in the sun and wind.

Fred's the first of the pair
His lower trunk reveals a large, open wound
The size of a ripe watermelon
Fred is aging a bit faster than his bride
Turning red and glowing like a Superstar.

By his side I spot Betsy
I wink at her
For her limbs are in fine fettle
Trimmed in luxuriant yellow and gold.

Betsy has been Fred's help
Through the lean years since his accident
Encouraging him, soothing him, giving and forgiving
Loyal, steadfast, committed to Fred for life.

I visit with Fred and Betsy
And they smilingly share all their stories with me
I begin to reflect on life and its twists and turns.

Thankful to this faithful couple, I will now join
My friends to romp ten miles
Up, down, up, up, up again
Through Morgantown.

With spirit uplifted, once more I bid a heartfelt
Thanks to Fred and Betsy
And they, in return, reply,
"Vaya con Dios!" to me.

I will try now to soak in
This delicious day
To share, to run, to shout with joy
The lilting melody of celebration!

So long, Fred and Betsy. I love you!
But, above all, enjoy this day
So richly given to us.

Welcome, Autumn!

Sun in my face, wind through my hair
Filled with God's grace, chill in the air
This is the season I love the best
Not much more mowing, time for some rest.

Thoughts turn to homecoming, marathons, more
Son's off to school, bringing friends in the door
Nothing, no, nothing can equal the fall
When fast times abound and training's a ball.

Why, just this morning thought I, "This is funny,"
As donning a jacket, I said bye to my honey
Hadn't worn long sleeves in many a moon
Hey, this October feels better than June.

No more of July when the heat penetrated
I'll not miss August, which made me slow-gaited
Now as the colors around us do turn
We'll find once again we have much speed to burn.

It's recharged my body, it's massaged my soul
I relish sweet cider, popcorn by the bowl!
O Autumn, dear memories I pray thou will make
With friendship aplenty as each step I take.

———•+•+•———

Sunsweet September Memories

Soaking in the rays, the muscles unwind
The voice of His wisdom I'm seeking to find
The training run's over, the hill's pain is past
Just what did I see that is destined to last?

At the end of the trek by the side of the road
Walking, I'd lightened the bulk of my load
When I spotted two butterflies yellow and gold
I stopped and I watched their sad story unfold.

It seemed that they were husband and wife
Or in any event faithful lovers for life
The male fluttered 'round his sweetheart with fire
But she sidestepped 'tween gravels and seemed so to tire.

His heart didn't accept what she tried hard to tell
That she couldn't answer his lively love bell
A speeding car, caring not a good whit
Had mortally struck and her body had hit.

She tried hard to tell him, "O true one, my dear,
I think it's too late and old death's sting is near
Kiss me, hold me gently, it is thou whom I love
But leave in a moment, we'll rejoin up above."

I did not stay watching as the play ran its course
For I couldn't bear sorrow and loss at the source
I am grateful for sunshine, for yesterday's race
For my wife, for this meal, and most for God's grace.

But seeing the butterflies made me aware
How precious each day is, creation we share
Thanks for endurance at September fast race
And for the fellowship 'fore and after the pace.

The crickets are chirping as nightfall comes near
And birch leaves are silent, no rustle I hear
There's reason for hope when we see morning break
And we're thankful this day, make no mistake.

The Smell of Walnuts
and a Bluebird's Call

Autumn's chill ran with me this morning
A bright, bright, sunshiny day
An array of colors you couldn't imagine
Well worth the eight miles invested.

I run now with pain
In two days the surgeon will set the date
To repair the second hernia in five years
And I'll be grounded from my beloved running.

So, realizing this,
Every run I take, indeed I cherish
Best aroma award today goes to the black walnuts.

As I approached a grove of trees
The north wind whooshed their fragrance to me
And I immediately pictured a plate of brownies
Or walnut cake with penuche icing – a huge hunk.

But on the ledger's other side
Today I spotted a bluebird near my trail
Who had lost to the highway's hurrying monsters
While harvesting seeds for winter nourishment.

The numbers mounted – bluebirds three
I cried a lot inside as I thought
Of the stupidity and cruelty of man
And how hard it is to be a bird,
A beast, a child –
In this twisted age.

At least out here, on the road
I feel an affinity with all creation
A natural fellow whose creed is "Live and let live!"
Doing some roadwork/roadplay
To prepare for what will be his last race
For a while.

So, "Carpe diem!" Seize the day!
Rejoice along with me
The countless bluebirds sing their songs
And walnut smells are free!

Cruising with the Crickets

In early September I try to remember
The reasons why I run
What is glad, what is bad, and everything
That makes it so much fun.

The long, long jaunts are history now
Charleston, P-burg, and Wheeling
And with grateful heart and a yen for the chill
A joy for the autumn I'm feeling.

You can have your summer runs
Long faces wrapped in sweat
But give me a race on the dew-laden turf
With cider and donuts – and the best times yet.

America is back again
Of marathon victory we have the scents
For at Tokyo's championship
Prevailed our own Steve Spence.

And of his mettle many more
Stand ready in the wings
Whether Curp or Taylor, magician or sailor,
One may earn Barcelona's rings.

The day is winding down tonight
I think about the fall
The leaves, the pumpkins, chopping wood
Indeed I have a ball!

This week was a 5K
Great Race is a 10
Cumberland's a fleet 15
And Morgantown's a win
(At least for the challenging terrain and
beautiful hot-air balloon festival!)

The crickets outside are calling me,
"Come out and hit your stride,"
With frost on our shoes or wind in our face
We're winners as long as we've tried.

The 1991 Parkersburg Half-Marathon

August 17 and a really great race
In just five years moving from infancy to richness
Some 1,400 toed the starting line, a national championship
Competition especially keen – deep, deep fields.

Mama Cass would call this morn
"Such a summer's day" – like, man, A.O.K.
A cool breeze prevailed, runners truly sailed
A splendid day emerged as the "Jon and Olga Day."

Jon Sinclair worked his magic
Taking turns sharply, knowing where his fellow eagles stood
In endurance, stamina, and heart,
Young Reyes and Espinosa gave their all
But Jon's last surge held them off by mini-seconds,
What a finish!

Olga took it out hard 'tween miles two and three
And Diane, Mary, and Janis hung on valiantly
Not to be denied, Olga sped along
And edged Diane's best ever with a course record
Of her own.

What can one say to describe all its glory?
Fun, fellowship, excellence – in abundance is the story
If you've not raced it, next year's just fine
Good times await you when you toe the line.

Before the Shower – January First

After running much less and many holiday fests
With plate piled up high (I almost turned into a pie!)
The scales did not lie, so I said with a sigh,
"Gotta hit the road or be mistaken for a bloated toad."

Marty and I had gotten in late
From an incomparable New Year's Eve date
The star of the music show had called me to the stage
And in "playing" lead guitar, as in running,
I did not act my age (not even remotely).

Removing confetti from clothing and hair
We said thanks to the piano man
And took our leave there
We toasted with Swiss and purple vina
Commenced sleeping at two
And waking at eight, my day seemed brand new.

I batched whole wheat pancakes for me and my gal
Looked at the bland list of Bowl games
And said, "Oh, wow,"
Scheduled my run in my mind's eye for one
Then did a few errands and jobs just for fun.

Basically, the run was good and I was slow
But I made my goal, my face did glow
Almost six miles mayn't seem like much to thee
However, in my "resting" time I've done just four or three.

At 4.2 I found some lady's keys on the edge
Of the road
Will do detective work, get them back to her,
Perhaps ease her load
Two iced-cold soft drinks later, I really feel calm
While Marty batches me some lunch and plays the role of mom.

Head really itches, the muscles fatigue
A runner's a hero in anyone's league
I'm closing in soon on my three hundredth race
From spirited sprints to treks of slow pace.
The running clothes, heavy, go from wash cycle to spin
I'm in uncommonly good shape for the shape I am in
As new year arises, I am truly blessed
Hot shower, do soak me; yes, running's the best.

Hooked

Some people may live for football
Or to swim in the blazing sun
But for me the sport that beats all
Is, yahoo, you guessed it, the run.

When I first really started in '78
I was slow, no endurance, a "tramp"
Who would have guessed that in just a few years
I'd be solid and sleek, well, a champ!

Who'd ever dream that this same spunky guy
Would complete two marathons without batting an eye?
But he caught on as time rolled along
That running's what gives him the spring in his song.

He tries to keep running in kilter
With other key aspects of life
And running does offer the filter
Decreasing frustrations and strife.

This bright and blue November day beckons me out the door
And I truly know without a doubt just what today is for
This guy was made for running, a happy wanderer he,
And as my body glides along, I wave to all I see.

November Winds

O winds of November, you carry me home
You soar like my spirit, right close to the dome
And though I well know there are raw days ahead
I thank thee for all as I kneel by my bed.

Another year running has quickly sped by
The beautiful memories, oh my, oh my!
From autumn 'til summer a trail always beckons
The heart ever restless, the quiet mind reckons.

The long chill of winter will rattle our bones
Testing our mettle, will alter our tones
But knowing the hardships that dot running's way
We'll muster the courage to reach spring's new day.

October's first race was in Cumberland fair
And the good times we had were beyond compare
A 15K battle from Mount Savage down
It leveled, rose upward, then careened into town.

Maryland hospitality was really, well, ample
Of food, drink, and laughs we had more than a sample
The K of C hall down the street held our party
And with Wilma and Mike conversation was hearty.

The tenth month flowed on, to Columbus we sped
And as race volunteers watered many a head
Their marathon truly is one of the best
They've added a 10K that many does test.

The days how they shorten, oh where have they flown?
A time to reflect, whom we love, how we've grown,
To live each day boldly from wire to wire
Sharing popcorn and laughter on a rug by the fire.

Rainy Friday Night

"What's new?" you ask
As here on the sofa I bask
Clad in pajamas at only 8:30
Is that middle age creeping in?
Or just the life of Riley? (or Garfield, for you youngsters).

I can hear the cars sloshing by on the road out front
I think I hear a rumble of thunder
Down on the rushing Ohio River
Tummy's full from four chocolate chip-oatmeal
Cookies served warm from the oven.

Public radio's sending in everything from jazz
To twanging guitars and synthesizers
Looking for a new job is going well
Son will decide where he'll begin college
In the fall, and running's a ball.

Last two times on the training route
Have revealed some improved speed
(I knew there was plenty of room for that!)
A Dixieland band is now belting out
"Sweet Georgia Brown," so hum or sing a few bars with me
And I'll dribble or twirl the roundball
Like Goose Tatum or Meadowlark Lemon.

Knowing that spring showers were on the way,
Earlier this week I completed my orchard
(If some year all of them bear, I'm in big trouble)
But planting a tree is like starting a race
It takes a heap of faith.

I'm strongly attracted to planting trees
And gardens – and running
Some days they put a smile on a frowning face
Today I crafted a large basket of pansies
For a neighbor, just home from the hospital.

You know, I'll consider myself the luckiest man
(Or blessed, to be more accurate)
If tomorrow I can just arise from restful sleep
And walk around house and yard;
To be able to run is ecstasy.

Planted more asparagus and rhubarb this week
It's a good, positive feeling to be out there
And, hey! Upper body work begins in earnest
Next week with our favorite – grass mowing!

Would you please pass me four more cookies.

October Magic

There's magic in the air today in Morgantown
In myriad majesty a never-ending flock
    of hot-air balloons float northward toward Pennsylvania.

My ears are pleasantly tickled by the dependable sounds
    of these multi-colored beauties
Yellows, greens, oranges, blues, silvers, golds, purples –
    why, every shade of the rainbow and more,
But none surpassing God's hues I saw yesterday
    in maple, sweet gum, dogwood, and oak.

What a delicious day!
One for early rising and living to the hilt!
Soon where I sit will be filled with runners
Going ten tough miles toward a finish line
    inside a football stadium.

Far better to be a runner of distances
    than to be confined to a football field
Now locked for security reasons.

Far better to race with relaxed arms,
Unencumbered by fences and locks,
Sharing joy and fellowship with
    brother and sister runners,
The pre-race pasta dinner, and after the race –
    dry clothes, refreshing water, juices, fruit. *That's* paradise!

This day I know I can soar with eagles
And feel like those pioneers up, up, and away in balloons,
Grateful and thankful to our Maker.

"Whoosh! Whoosh!" I hear more balloonists ascending,
Time to go. Catch you at the finish line, friend, I trust.
"Vaya con Dios!"

Return to Glory

'Twas yesterday and, boy, was I psyched
While playing the oldies into Athens I hiked
In white station wagon I arrived at the race
And scores of fine memories flooded brain, soul, and face.

Nine whole years had whisked by and gone
Since '85, the time of my first marathon
I'd run hot, I'd run slow, but had finished the course
Where I beamed ear to ear though my body felt worse.

It's good to be early, I toned to myself
And double-tied laces, best shoes from the shelf
I felt well nourished and certainly no thinner
For last night I'd polished off pizza and pecan rolls
After a king-sized pasta dinner.

The morning was cool, so I opted for gloves
And bedazzling neon yellow shorts, one of my loves
With an Etonic Racing Team singlet at crest of top layer
I knew in a moment it was great being there.

The old courthouse clock chimed the hour of high noon
And I thought we'd be bookin' outta there pretty soon,
I found front row spot on this brick field of dreams
Might as well go first class, more fun, so it seems.

I turned right to a friend and said, "Go get em, Mitch!"
He returned the same, then we're off without a glitch
We chewed up brick streets, three in fact, and then hit the mile
She barked, "7:11!" my heart lit up all the while.

I had fun, plenty of it, but did change my game plan
Didn't do the whole course but felt no less a man
In half-marathon this time I ran five decent miles
Then retraced my steps, flashing warm, gentle smiles.

Had to tell the water stops politely,
"Nope, I'm not the leader,
Just out for a training run,"
They grinned and gave me all I needed.

The bonus of this little switch did blossom very soon
 As leading runner in the race sped by like cow on moon
I learned humility right then and there
It was poetry in motion, yup, I know that life's not fair.

So as I jogged pleasantly back
I helped out a little the top twenty in the pack
Told each his position and what was coming behind
And thought of the leader, whose speed made me blind.

Back at the stadium dry togs I put on
Soon oranges and glasses of orange drink were gone
The sun shone brightly as we waited for the first marathoner
I readied my camera, considering the honor.

Guess who it was? You're right, Mitch from the start
And Mitch Bentley, though hobbling, had won it with heart,
They placed laurel wreath 'round his head with great care
We returned, yes, to glory, that April day there.

Redbud, Dogwood, and Hope Renewed

You never can tell
When you take a run
What's gonna happen
Nope, you never can tell.

The low pressure lifted, the rain slipped away
Ol' Sol started boiling, I was off on my way
The first four-tenths up took in a mean hill
But it will pay off in Wheeling, it will, oh it will.

The grandeur of springtime 'came etched in my soul
And bathing my spirit, did make me feel whole
Wind in my face and flowers all around
Spellbound in dreamland, I made not a sound.

My well-weathered Brookses just ate up the route
And 'bout this world's conflicts I cared not a hoot
The champion performers numbered just two
Redbud and dogwood, the proud and the few.

After forty-some minutes I eased to a halt
Walked the last mile home, I could fly, I could vault
To add to the splendor of this afternoon
Came a swallowtail butterfly
I could swear this is June.

You know, there's somethin' special
In these nature tromps we take
The energies that we invest
Strike "gold," for goodness sake.

And as I here at gardenside
Watch miracles unfold
I think of love and running
Dogwoods, redbuds make me bold.

Others may not understand it
But it is we who count
We can only hope they'll join us
And drink freely from the fount.

Smelling the Roses

Rain begins, it pitters, it patters, it teases
But it's acomin', that's for sure
I was semi-soaked this morning
As the sprinklers "upstairs" made test patterns on asphalt.

Ah, what a glorious workout it was
Five and a half miles on roly-poly Route 3
The "Robert Jones of Running" must have designed it
For it offers every challenge and enjoyment known.

Wasn't hustling super fast, so was surprised
When ye olde timepiece displayed 40:27
Why, just a week ago we were talking 43
It's mysterious; is it middleaged second wind
Or is it training and nutrition?
I certainly will not unduly question or analyze.

The Huntington race made me blue in the face
Wind chill 25 degrees effectively did jawbone freeze
Ten miles 'cross bridges by Ohio River side
Made this journey tougher than many I've tried.

But it was a grand one, and hundreds attended
Elite runners everywhere, the list never ended
We had lots of fun, Dean Reinke was there
And Cabell Huntington Hospital had an A-plus health fair.

Well, back to the future, the next race is Wheeling
I don't have to tell you how sore I'll be feeling
But I do recommend this four-hill course
As it seems custom-made for a Roughrider's horse.

I look to the north over garden and yard
And the poetry's out there, I feel like the Bard
The cumulo-nimbus are on the increase
Run slow, smell the roses, laugh hard, I shall cease.

Prime Thoughts
and Magic

Every day I run I'm a brand new me
The earth greets the sun, and the run is free
And as the wind goes whistling along
In rhythmical flight I sing many a song.

The hills beckon to me, they come and they go
And some days I'm fast while on others I'm slow
But always a smile punctuates my tan face
I'm pleased to be out there, to be one of the race.

This runnin' has hooked me, a goner for sure
And while I am here, I'm all sweaty and pure
I scan latest listings of upcoming races
And think of good times, ample food, friendly faces.

I'll try hard this year to take running in stride
To keep it in balance and fun at my side
No matter what life dares to throw in my way
I'll endure and finish, running's built me to stay.

Every moment I run, every week, every year
I will soak in the flavor, cast aside any fear
Grateful I'm out there, some days fast, others slow
Touching the miracles as onward I go.

A Runner's Weather Report

In these dusty summer dog days, answers hard to find
I turn to thoughts of spirit to help refresh my mind
I see the towering thunderheads now building in the west
And marvel at their mighty power and give my pen a rest.

Somehow a shaft of sunset has hit the leading cloud
On top left side 'bout ten o'clock, it looks both pure and proud
The second cloud in quick pursuit, shaped like a warrior bold
Fumanchu beard and flowing locks, a story to be told.

Now I have a profile of relentless Fumanchu
His contorted face is straining like runners me and you
And right behind his giant sculpt the lightning flashes form
The night will host an awful storm, a respite from the warm.

A glowing peachy orange has oozed all through our runner's hair
Cloud three emerges from its home, why, a minute ago it wasn't there
It was a snake, shook off its tail, resembles Daffy Duck
If I describe another cloud, you'll say, "What's wrong, o dreamer Chuck?"

Night fell and we were eager as we waited for the storm
Replete with dazzling fireworks, the sky was true to form
So off we dozed in humid air, poised so for winds on high
Sparse raindrops pulled their vanishing act and merely passed us by.

Although the air is parched and dry, the temperatures are dandy
The breeze is up, and off I go on any run that's handy
Training harder for what's next, just twenty days from now
The championship half-marathon, golleee and holy cow!

Just as the rain did pass us by, why, change is all we have
And even on the best of days keep close bandaids and salve
But we have power within us to turn a blue day brighter
And don't forget the more you run, why, you're a better fighter.

There're many ways to "skin a cat," to have a fresh perspective
So go for acts that give you joy, be they sprightly or reflective
And as the days lead on to years, on sunny ones or damp
The more you give, the more you'll live, in harmony – a champ.

What a View !

I'm the tape and the finish at the end of the run
Where the work is now over, and it's time for some fun
I see everyone scurrying by
And they all have their stories, so to tell them I'll try.

Here comes the champ as he bursts through with ease
He's young, he trains hard, and his times surely please
A modest man he and a gentleman, too
A model to follow for me and for you.

And here's the first woman, she's running so well
There are plenty more like her, swift and clear as a bell
To see them in shape and having such fun
Wins other girls over, says running's the one.

Then there's that kid, it's his very first race
I can read that wide grin spread across his glad face
He's proud that he's done it, for it was quite hard
To run the whole race, not just lounge in a yard.

The much older lady, the older man, too
True stories of courage, of comebacks anew
Recovering from illness, a new lease on life
A passionate fire propels joy over strife.

So, what I'm a saying as I look back your way
Is I'm glad that you're out here, having much fun today
For you're all important in the great scheme of things
The victor's wreath yours, and Olympian rings.

Ode to Number Ten

O trusty companions, without you I'm bare
You keep me a moving, going here, going there
I chase up tall hills and cross valleys below
And in your sweet grip it's a running I go.

You soak up the moisture from snow and from rain
And given a choice, why, you'd do it again
You smile and say "Ahh" when you're propped up to dry
As if to say thanks, nodding off with a sigh.

We're a proud family, brothers, sisters, a team
The room where you live, eating cookies and cream
Just relaxing to vibes on your many days off
While I alternate pairs, don't be jealous, don't scoff.

I'm proud of you all, deep devotion I give
For you're heart and soul of the way that I live
It's you I depend on oft times in the race
To "kick in" a sprint or to just up the pace.

You'll always be with me 'til running is through
We're size tens forever, brand new to shoe goo
Of shouts, sweats, and singlets other runners may boast
But you, loyal friends, are the ones I love most.

The World of a Chaise Lounge

I'm white and burgundy brown, you see
    And there's this runner a sittin' on me
Takin' a break from the heat of the day
    So I'll just prod him to see things *my* way.

Chuck, my boy, don't you know the score?
    Too much workin' will make you sore
Please lean back easy – relax, relax
    And I'll help you 'preciate life to the max.

See the swallows, dive bombers all
    And the cardinals out there, having a ball
Harvesting seeds from the 'ol compost heap
    So graceful, such beauty, they lull you to sleep.

And the breeze is up – hear it?
    (You runners like that!)
It flutters the birch leaves
    Gives me a cool pat
There's nothing, no, nothing, like the wind in your face
It speaks of life's miracles, and that's no disgrace.

Gaze on the sunset, lad, indeed take it in
For there's more here than runnin' (if you lose, if you win)
The days roll on so swiftly, and hairs turn quickly gray,
So daily smell more roses, and give yourself to play.

This runnin' makes ye happy? Indeed it does seem so
So you just keep on keeping on – be ye fast or be ye slow
And live each day right to the hilt, seek joy whate'er betides
And be the best that you can be, I dub thee Prince of Strides.

Amish Soul

The twelfth broke oh so chilly
On that special April morn
But warmed to racing fever
As at noon the race was born.

A horde of lean and not so lean
Sped on at cannon's blast
A motley crew of runners fair
Some swift, some not so fast.

Greeting us were many moos
From cows that lined the course
"There's Elsie! I swear 'tis she"
She's saluting, "Go with the Force."

Pungent scents from countryside
Kept us wide awake
"It's not so bad," (I lied, I lied)
"As chicken or piggy, for goodness' sake."

We passed the mile marks one by one
As Strasburg greeted us
And turned us 'round toward Lancastertown
Without a peep or fuss.

At ten or eleven our bodies protested
As fun became more of a chore
Why, out stepped a piper in kilt well adorned
And kindled the music for more!

One detail in common with previous years
Was a stiff breeze right out of the north
Near twelve I tried hard to "draft" off a pard
But failed, said, "So long,"
And, with third wind or fifth, scurried forth.

Nothing's so dear as the ol' golfing course
For you know that the finish is near
Why, they're snapping your picture as you try to look sharp
But, oh, no, one more hill's there, I fear.

Dinner bell rings at Lancastertown
As runners respond to the call
Carrying platters so heaped which will lull them to sleep
And a good time is had by them all.

As this runner stoked his trusty "stove"
With ice cream sandwiches
(the hostess smiled and gave me an endless supply)
I thought of the fun, cows, and gentle Amish folks,
When she grinned, "Have another?"
"I'll try."

23:05

I didn't really push a lot
'Twas just a little Turkey Trot
Mile 'n a half out, mile 'n a half back
'Nough to work up a lather, Jack.

Local boy home from Marshall sped
To win the race (he always led)
I saw Christy ahead of me
Blonde ponytail bouncing, she smiled with glee.

As I neared the turn, the leaders rushed toward
Coming right by me, not saying a word
I told young Randy, "Looking good, looking good!"
He smiled with a twinkle, as I knew he would.

On the hundred-yard stretch I let it all out
But whether I'd catch 'em, I did have a doubt
They had help pace me three quarters or so
But I had plenty left, nothin' personal, ya know?

The liquid refreshments trickled down a cold chin
And I felt I'd run well for the shape I was in
The Turkey Trot's over, next, Snowflake Chase
And there's nothing, no, nothing, like running a race.

The Wall

The wall said April second
But it sure a foo-led me
For the stinging snow it pelted
As I planted cherry tree.

My body still is frozen
From a race called "Cooper's Rock"
Where four days ago my body
Was just drenched from cap to sock.

So, on this day I ponder
Where to run and how to train
While the snowflakes become prisms
And dazzle eye and brain.

Will I run the Amish Marathon
On Ap-a-ril the twelfth?
Or will I respect this sneeze and cough
And just-a- jog, regain my health?

'Ol moderation's creeping in
I hear its windy roar
Nothing to prove in marathons
I've been there twice before.

And then the Charleston 15-Miler
I've chugged it seven times
Those hills are growin' steeper
And a little hard to climb.

But there's a glint of hope left
In this runner still not fat
I continue turning races down
That are too straight or flat.

I still like the challenge
Of a curvy, rambling course
Though my afterburners
Don't "kick in" with Spence's force.

Every race I enter
Is a Barcelona day
And I think we'd all be smarter
If we spent more time at play.

So as I look at calendar
In place upon the wall
I smile and think of running friends, of cherry trees and fall.

Flash!

Took a run just yesterday
    Ran four miles in the usual way
Watch didn't lie, said I was fast
    Felt grand and wanted the day to last.

But it didn't, you see, it whirled on by
    A new one's here, new dreams to try
Adventure calls, it beckons well
    If we say no, no one will tell.

The truth sublime is on a roll
    Although the years will take their toll
We've ample time to make our mark
    To give some back, ignite a spark.

Though it goes fast, the time is now
    To stretch our wings and pledge our vow
Say "yes" to life and savor all
    Too soon will come the hint of fall.

So, "Pop, pop, pop!" the camera goes
    The lights explode, so does the rose
Its petals perfect fade and die
    Enjoy today; I do not lie.

You comfort me in the valleys and give me strength.

Beauty is truth; truth, beauty
That is all ye know on earth and all ye need to know.

John Keats

———●•••●———

Evening Reflections

Meditations that are sober
As clock turns to October
It's a long way through the winter
Light lessens to a splinter.

I'm counting on you, running,
To get me through
To keep me in some balance
And faith and strength renew.

It's been a glorious summer
I'm running really well
And I count ample blessings
So grand they ring the bell!

Father, keep alive in me
A childlike sense of wonder
To keep me warm when days are dreary
And the world seems especially out of step.

Create in me a wholesome spirit
Ready always to give and give and share
Help me to look for good in other folks
To seek out and enjoy fellowship
With brother and sister runners huddling
'Round a roaring fire with snow
And 20 degrees, amid the Savage River pines.

We are so fortunate to be runners
Help me to live one day at a time.

The Long Road Back

I don't feel very creative today
But at least I'm going to try
The warm breath of April has eased into this February day
And I am glad to be part of it on my run.

You see, I'm battling an old nemesis, depression
And it's no picnic, to say the least
The moods and feelings swing all over the place
You know you're O.K., but you feel like a disgrace.

I don't really feel like running
For the muscles aren't working so well
But I make myself run, for a runner I am,
And any small goal accomplished on the roads
Can help rebuild my shaky confidence.

Medicines do work, but they take time
And running is wonderful therapy
I sense that the strength is returning
And I am grateful for this sport that keeps me going.

I've come through some upsets, as folks sometimes do
And one day at a time faith will carry me through
For all of us journey the long road back now and then
And he who keeps trying is the one who will win.

———

Mercurial

February in its many moods
    Radical from day to day
Balmy sixties yesterday
    Today snow slaps me in the face.

Stronger strides, I float along
    I'm happy here and sing my song
Vaulting puddles, I jump for joy
    King of the road, this lucky boy.

The miles whisk by, and races beckon
    Their torrid pace will hurt, I reckon
But that's a part of living still
    The race's not won 'til you climb the hill.

My total's up, each day increasing
    Each year my love burns hot, unceasing
After the run, the soothing walk
    Peer 'cross the lake, admire the hawk.

Pick up tossed cans, make litter-free
    A highway fit for you and me
My days may vary, low to high
    But I'll court running 'til I die.

To Running

Running, how do I thank thee?
You keep me going when going is tough
You give me strength and courage
When the valleys and shadows deepen.

Much as I love you, many days I have to force myself
To begin my run
But after I've hung in there for awhile
I'm grateful and proud to be running.

Thou art my rod and staff,
You discipline me, you give me goals
You strengthen me to carry on, to have faith
In times of severe testing.

There was a hint of spring yesterday
As I ran in the rain for six miles
And I hope for spring's return 'ere long
And to be born again like tulips and daffodils.

Winter blues are hard to fight
Perhaps they are for you
But with friend Running at our side
We know we'll make it through.

Almost Spring

March five
Feeling stronger, it's good to be alive
Any 'ol ailment will run its course
And I soon may resemble a frisky horse.

Snow crystals pelted from a staunch wind west
And I headed northward, the back road, the best
The first mile clicked off, it wasn't so hard
And my mind paused to ponder as I passed Chloe's yard.

Then wending on along the way, where were they? Oh, gee, darn!
I guess my two horse buddies were lounging in a barn
The sheep, likewise, were partying in their pad
And missing them, I felt just a little "baaad"!

Well, up and down and level off I heard a bark or two
Of hounds, mutts, and retrievers – why, they like running, too
Yup, there they were in yards, tied up, not free
And here I was, king of the road, oh, yes, I'm glad I'm me.

Today I didn't quite make my mileage goal
But not to worry, I'm feeling whole
Wasn't able to run the Half-Marathon at Williamsburg
But will go the same distance one day past April third.

At the site, Athens, Ohio, there was a mighty roar
Recalling the '85 Marathon, oh, was I stiff and sore!
I'll dedicate this run to Troy Organ, philosopher and friend
And I'll be glad it's just a half as I approach the end.

The joy of writing has returned in cozy rocking chair
And if I mind my P's and Q's, I'll soon be running fair
The birds chirp lustily, "Have faith, plant more fruit trees"
And I reply, "I will, I will!" as one more day I seize.

Rainy Day Pizza Popping

Sitting by the jukebox in a little pizza place
    The rain pours down in buckets, why, it spatters on my face
Dreams of coming races bring a smile upon my brow
    But this morning's meditations ask just why and never how.

Gotta keep my wits about me, realize the truth in man
    All's a mystery for certain, few things follow mortal plan
Gotta grab for goals and laughter, gotta do what pleases me
    For the rest is savage strangeness, few who care,
      And few who see.

Make the active life my brother, do what inner yearnings bid
    Offer up my all to being, keeping open, never hid
Realizing that not many will elect to join my ship
    Keep a guard on criticizing, more on listening, less on lip.

I'm at home, the pizza eaten, post hole dug, a muddy mess
    This is really how I like life; keep it simple, I confess
Four more days 'til Athens race time, may God grant me many more
    Lift my hymn of thanks to skyward; grant me courage, I implore.

Veritas

I met Truth again today
Out in the open season
With the wind wild and playful
I marvelled at its majesty.

Much, methinks, from day to day
Is filled with sham and appearance
What passes for normality
Is groupthink and mediocrity.

Thankful hearts we raise to thee,
O Father!
For the special gift of thy hand, running,
Thou hast given to all of us as your children.

Clear, serene, better able to persevere
That's how I feel after I meet thee
Refreshed, cleansed, annoying thoughts scattered away
A potentially new, loving person in soggy shoes.

The beauty of being in motion
Playing with speed, alternately relaxing and building
Perhaps Solomon found morsels of wisdom in running
Do we commune with Whitman
As we glide over the trail's turf, the leaves of grass?
Do we breathe in the understanding of Thoreau
As our paths lead on past pond, lake, or stream?
Do we soak it all in, simplicity, a radiant beam?

Let us gird our loins with strength and character
So that we will run and not be weary
So that our actions will show we practice truth in love
Veritas, thy very name is noble and pure.

The quest

The best-laid schemes o' mice an' men
gang aft agley (often go astray).

Robert Burns

First Marathon

Today is January 6. I ran 4.2 miles this chilly morning. For therapy, you might say. I'm fighting an ailment called depression. I'm seeing a counselor every two or three weeks, and we talk about how best to solve the problems. But I feel best when I'm out running.

Now I'm no great runner. But I seem to be getting better and faster at it. I started distance running in November of 1978 with a 5K run and have become more serious at it during the last two years or so. I've won age-group awards, and my times at various distances are coming down.

My longest run was 15 miles last Labor Day weekend. I finished within four minutes of the goal I had set.

The straw that nearly "broke" this camel's back occurred in late October. I work as a teacher and had been serving as assistant athletic director during most of my eight years at this particular high school.

The principal called me into his office. "Chuck," he said, "you've blown it. Scalping tickets has cost you your athletic director's job."

Well, I didn't exactly consider what I had done scalping tickets. A student had walked up to me during my planning period and asked if her aunt could buy one of my three season tickets (with two or three home games remaining) since her aunt sat right behind our assigned seats and knew we hadn't been using them. (We hadn't been using them because her aunt and her aunt's friend both are incessant cigarette smokers, and I detest smoke). So I said, "I guess so," and took the ten dollars she handed me. That's not exactly my concept of "scalping" tickets, but the end result was that the principal's mind was made up, and I resigned from the position effective a few days later.

Losing the position was an immense blow to my feelings of human dignity, and our school district hummed with stories that probably stretched the truth and pegged me as a fellow who had swindled hundreds of fans with high-priced tickets for the "big game." To me the punishment didn't fit the "crime," and I harbored much anger and felt my reputation had been unjustly injured.

My wife (Martha) urged me to see a psychologist, so when our first winter snow hit and school was cancelled one day in early December, I made an appointment. My counselor's name was Mike, and I told him that I didn't think I could make it past the end of the first semester as a teacher. Mike helped me to sort out some of the feelings I had and to analyze my choices and look toward the future.

Just before school ended for Christmas, the principal called me in for my fall evaluation as a teacher. He didn't emphasize anything that I was doing well but picked on a few things that I didn't do his way. At this point my anger was still pretty great, but I maintained my composure.

On my second visit with Mike he asked if I still wanted to take some time off from teaching at the end of the first semester. I said yes, so I signed a release form for him to share his opinions with my family medical doctor, who might have to justify my absence from work.

Anyway, over the holidays my body told me that dropping out was not so good. I felt tightness in my head, not all the time, but fairly often.

School resumed on January 3. During December I ran about 75 miles, an increase for me over my usual monthly total. The first week of January I ran 29 miles. My thoughts were these: my stamina and speed are both increasing. The weight is steady at 155, and my dream is to complete my first marathon on April 14 in Athens, Ohio. With God's help I will do it. I'm not as sure about my ability to complete the rest of the school year unscathed without an extended absence or a lot of little absences. I have my résumé in order and have applied in the past month for four positions that appear to be satisfying. I've taken a Strong-Campbell Interest Inventory to help me re-evaluate what my main interests are. I have lots of talent but feel like a round peg in a square hole. So much of the joy and freedom is being taken out of high school teaching and learning these days, at least at our school. And I'm big on joy and freedom! That's why I'm a runner. I love the pure, sublime feeling of flowing over the roads or paths, even at my average pace. I love the communion with nature and self that running affords.

January 10. Lots to report today. First, two days ago I ran a personal best on my 4.2-mile hilly route. Had on my new runner's I.D. necklace given to me by a student I've been tutoring at his home. The run felt quite good, and I really wasn't pushing it.

Also yesterday was cool. Had a comfortable day at work even with the seven classes to guide and then to preside over our Fellowship of Christian Athletes meeting. At four I had my third chat with Mike. Told him I felt stronger, was pacing myself at work, and felt confident that I had enough creative ideas and stamina to finish the "race" to the end of the school year. He said to keep running and that he enjoyed watching the Athens Marathon each year near his home.

Today schools were called off because of a few inches of snow. I needed a workout, however. Did four miles up our county road and back eight times. Monotonous? Heck, no! I was too busy listening for cars when I'd have to leave the one clear path in the middle for the snow-covered lanes. Kept a steady pace.

Runner magazine arrived in the mail. A superb issue, including lots of ideas on new races to enter. I'd better start saving that extra coin for transportation to all these places where I'd like to run. Great article that you wrote, George Sheehan! Sorry I didn't take the time to meet you up close and personal at the Charleston (WV) Distance Run. You had a great race! I've been reading a good book today, too. Hope that snow doesn't stick around too long. Need to get some longer runs in this week, and the main road's just a bit too treacherous when snowy, even with my balance and agility.

January 23. Boy, did we have some blizzard conditions! When the Alberta clipper "clipped" Ohio, I curtailed the outdoor running. Caught a warm spell last Friday and ran our hilly, curving driveway hard for 15 minutes, anticipating a 3.5-mile race scheduled for Sunday. Whoops! Temperature dropped to -20 degrees F. with much wind, and the race was postponed.

Oh, yes. Yesterday was "D" (decision) day on the marathon. Completed the entry form for the Athens Marathon during my visit to the university where I received the results of that career interest inventory. The results made sense to me, and guess what, the counselor assisting me is a marathon runner. Good thing I didn't notice the bright marathon poster on a side wall of his office until fairly late in our visit, or we might have stayed on running as our central theme of conversation.

Today's temps were up near 30, so I logged a steady run of 8.2 miles. Lots of people wave and toot their horns in friendly fashion. Could it be that I'm a fixture on the training route? Brand new résumés are in use now, and I've applied for two interesting positions already. Guess which hobby heads the list of hobbies. Is it *running*? (Are Joe Montana and Dan Marino skilled quarterbacks?!)

February 3. To catch up on lots of news. For example, last Sunday the wintry weather cleared just enough for us to participate in the Super Sunday 5K Run in Parkersburg, beginning and ending on Broad Street hill by the YMCA. About 70 runners turned out on a cold afternoon to shuffle through the slush and snow. Saw several running friends before the race, and one fellow about my age asked if I thought I could run a 21-something today, sort of implying that he could. I replied, "Don't think so," knowing that the footing would be a bit tricky on the middle part of the course.

Anyway it was race time. I set up on the front line of runners, and over my left shoulder were Steve and Cliff Taylor, both the pride of St. Marys, West Virginia, and Steve a standout at WVU. We enjoyed a brief chat; then the starting commands were given. I got off well, and few runners passed me in the first mile after the initial surge in the first quarter mile.

At about 1.3 miles a superb runner, Ernie Doll, from Pennsboro edged ahead of me, but I felt good and smooth. At about 1.8 miles a very good woman runner caught me, but I stayed close and caught her back. She came ahead again, and I tucked in a few yards behind her. Still no other traffic was coming to me from behind. Great! With about a quarter mile to the finish line, I put on a sustained build and passed my friend just before we started the steep incline to the finish. I saw two runners up ahead and said to myself, "Why don't you see what you have left?" The answer was, "Plenty." Passed them with 15 yards to go and finished a decent 35th in a new personal best of 22:56. (I know that's not fast, but it's improvement nevertheless). Oh, by the way, Steve and Cliff finished 1-2 with Steve down around 14 minutes and a few seconds.

The weather turned wintry again by the middle of the week, but my January total miles met my goal for the month, and I had a good eight-mile run home from school where I left my workday clothes in a suitcase in the closet to change into my omnipresent bright orange and yellow attire, my trademark on Route 339.

I just finished a fantastic book called *Come Run with Me* by Peter Strudwick. It's a very heartwarming and courageous story of a marathon runner who has overcome rather formidable handicaps. Thanks, Pete!

Had a truly beautiful run this morning, nine miles, with the road cleared of snow just enough to render it fairly safe. The hardest training lies ahead, but the goal requires it. I have a better feeling about the options I'm considering for my next career. A sense of harmony is edging its way, slowly but surely, back into my life. Now to write a couple of letters, one to Mom and Dad and one to Sherry, my daughter. My, how swiftly the time flies. Sunrise, sunset – zip! They whiz by. Enjoy the days *deeply*.

February 14 – Happy Valentine's Day. Digging out from the biggest snow of the season. Just bathed after shoveling that long driveway of ours. After driving home from work on the twelfth I barely got in a 4.2-mile jaunt up to the lake and back on a roadway which was becoming slick on the edges. Have been re-reading Jim Fixx's book and that incomparable February edition of *Runner* to project mentally the races I'd like to try in 1985. Look out, Troy, Pennsylvania. Your barbecued ribs sound so mouthwatering and will make my day after your hilly trek in August! If this darned snow will beat a hasty retreat, I can get back to the road again. Two months from today is Marathon Day.

February 19 – In mid 30's and sunny today. I cracked out a new personal best on my l0K course. Wore no sweat bottoms today and felt strong on the run. Didn't see Mike on the thirteenth as I didn't see the need. Drove over to Athens and just happened to click on an impromptu interview for an enjoyable-looking position at the university.

February 24. Sunday night. What a week I've had! Should have known something good was going to happen when I set two personal bests at the 4.2-mile distance during training runs. The second PB didn't nip just a few seconds off the old PB but a whopping 79 seconds!

Then yesterday I had a two-hour drive each way to the 10K race northeast of Cambridge at Salt Fork Lake State Park. The course had lots of hills, but my time (sit down, now) was, yup, another PB by two minutes and 43 seconds. I finished back in 49th position but was quite happy with my time. I was steady and strong most of the way.

Wanted to run today, but Robbie (our ten-year-old) is coming to like tennis a lot, so before the rains started, we volleyed a half hour. I was glad we did. Tomorrow I'll be back to the longer distance run again.

March 3 – Another Sunday night. Ran eight miles yesterday and eight today. Became quite thirsty after 6½ miles. Stopped for four quick cups of water at the little corner store and took a fifth cup along with me. Met my goal for mileage for the month of February. Was ill last Friday and Saturday with an infection that took away most of my voice. Fortunately I had refills of two medicines left over from a similar infection last November.

I feel tired tonight. Will probably submit my letter resigning from my position this week or next. Learned to dislike some of those thoughtless drivers today. On three occasions two cars and a cycle passing other cars on our two-lane road came within two feet of squashing me even though I always run well to the left of the outside border line. Next race is a five-miler on March 16. I plan to win the prize for best costume in the Irish shamrock theme. Good night. Hope the energy returns tomorrow.

March 4 – Guess what? The energy returned. Knocked off a brisk 4.2 miles with the first half in near-record time. The return trip wasn't so great, but I was running directly into the teeth of 40-mph wind gusts. Temperature at this moment (5 P.M.) is 77 degrees, due to drop to the 20's (say what?!) tomorrow.

My sweet wife has some luscious turkey-biscuit casserole in the oven, and I have an "Anne Murray's Greatest Hits" tape on. Life is good. Drafted my letter today. Well, back to warmer tops for tomorrow's workout. March is as feisty as my brothers and I used to be in our adolescence. Thank you, God, for this body that so much enjoyed today's run, especially that first half with the wind of paradise at my back. Makes a fellow feel that he's soaring like an eagle.

March 14 – Gulp! Just one month until the Day! I've been running smoothly lately and am up to date on my schedule of gradually lengthening the mileage. Will take a break this Saturday to don my own creation of a St. Patrick's Day costume in a local five-mile run. I've opted for a brisk three-mile walk as I'll be weighted down with a tape player, blasting out spirited tunes and plaintive Irish melodies. That afternoon I'll do a ten-mile run, then 15 miles Sunday afternoon. Increase it by a little on each of three subsequent weekends, and I may have enough of the "right stuff" for Athens.

March 21 – Gee whillikers! Today found me in Athens, interviewing for a position which just became available at the university. I arrived home in time to do eight miles of training. Only three weeks and three days until the "Great Equalizer" gets its paws on me. Think marathon, Chuck, ol' boy.

Oh, by the way, I submitted my resignation from my teaching position exactly two weeks ago. With the break now made, I forge ahead and press onward to the goal of another niche for me.

I called Ryan Walters tonight, my #1 cross country runner on our conference championship team in '81. We relived old running memories.

March 24 – Sunday. I awakened at 6:04 this morning and saw that a clear, sunny day was beckoning, and I hit the trail for another longer run today, piggybacking on yesterday's 11-mile caper. That one started at 5:55, and, I must admit, there wasn't much light to guide my way for the first few miles.

Today's excursion was smooth and strong, only a minute or two slower than my PB at this distance. I was happy with it. Tomorrow I'd better put that shoe patch on the outside heels of three pairs of my runnin' shoes.

Had a narrow escape in the car today over in Athens with the family for dinner and taking first looks at possible houses. A little ol' lady ran a yield sign and nearly squashed a pleasant day for us. She missed us by inches.

March 31 – Wow! The time is flying. I rather enjoyed that long run in a steady downpour today. Kept a steady pace and knocked it off in an average of eight minutes and 44 seconds per mile. Took some water at eight and 13 miles. Am starting to figure out how much water is just right and when to slow down for it. Am reading Marc Bloom's book *The Marathon*. One more good, hard week of training; then it's time to slacken off gradually for the unforgiving distance of 26 miles, 385 yards. Boy, do I have an appetite these days! And the weight is that of high school days – 148 pounds. I finished 87th out of 150 runners in an extremely hilly 10K yesterday down at Charleston. It was the most enjoyable race I've yet entered.

Had a good time, running the last 4.2 miles side by side with a guy whom I helped through a stomach cramp as we came out of the steep part near the mountain top airport.

April 2 – After teaching seven classes, I played tennis for 20 minutes with Robbie, my ten-year-old son. Then he banged away at the wall while I "cooked" eight laps of the .8-mile local jogging path in a new personal best of 7.8 minutes per mile. The cool 40-degree temperature became chilly with the 20 mph wind out of the northwest. Will do a longer run tomorrow. I can almost feel the excitement of race day, and the adrenalin is flowing.

April 7 – Easter Sunday. I arose at 6:30 or so, read the paper quickly, then saw that the predicted second consecutive rainy Sunday was beginning with a light drizzle. In ten minutes I was off on my last long run over a hilly course, part of which consisted of new territory for me. I started at a pace a little slower than usual and felt stronger and steadier from the seven-mile mark 'til I brought it on home. The wool toboggan and dirty cotton gardening gloves kept me comfy, and the Columbia-blue jacket kept me quite dry. Bought a little container of Cold Duck in hopes of celebrating in a proper way the completion of this monumental task seven days from now. Began the carbohydrate binge in earnest today. Weight is at 148, a far cry from 162 last August and 169 in January of '84. I'll run up through and including Wednesday of this week. Then I'll give the ol' "equipment" a rest for the challenging terrain of Athens to Guysville and back. I feel that I can go the distance.

April 13 – Well, here we are, my wife Martha and I at a couples' seminar in Columbus. I took a few last looks at George Sheehan's *Running and Being* and had a pretty good night's rest. I know that I'll not sleep too soundly tonight with the marathon's being tomorrow. Still taking on water every chance that I have. Getting a little "edgy."

April 14 – Well, this is it, the day of reckoning. Slept very well last night, and that was a surprise. Little was I to know that a myriad of surprises lay ahead for me that day.

We left home for the site of the race about 10:05. The last breakfast was two slices of whole wheat toast, a cup of hot tea, a glass of orange juice, and vitamins B, C, and E.

At the county courthouse, adjacent to the starting line, I met a few of the runners who would go on the arduous adventure over the hills with me. There were Frank and Mel, who had driven all the way from western Iowa. There were many important persons whom I would meet later.

The race was imminent. We were given our final instructions, and a fellow on a unicycle (who would, incidentally, race the marathon as part of the uniqueness of this race) started down the brick streets of Athens. We followed at the sound of the gun, 146 strong.

I went out at about the pace I had planned. Some of the folks I met the first six or seven miles included Ron, a likeable attorney who, like the author, includes photography in his hobbies. There were Bob and John (father and son) and pleasant. Laura went by, a vivacious teacher of learning disabilities.

The course was an out-and-back loop. At about ten miles we started to encounter lots of hills, not all of them small. I peeled off my racing top and gave it to a race official coming by in a car. Draped the shirt over my back to cool that area if necessary later or to put back on the chest, for the sun was bearing down on me now. Humidity was 100%; and the temperature was at least 75 degrees, in a word, not your ideal day for a guy trying his first marathon. By the way, we were running directly into a 12-mph brisk wind.

I fell behind Ron, John, and Bob but didn't panic. I plodded steadily onward. Saw Professor Troy Organ, an experienced marathoner; even he was affected by the triple "H" – heat, humidity, and hills. Fortunately he recovered, and the last time I saw him, he had doubled back from the end of the loop and was looking smooth again and heading for the finish.

I hit the turn-around in 2:17, which wasn't far off the pace at which I was hoping to finish. But other tests lay ahead.

The most severe of the hills lay between miles 10 and 15, and they took their toll. By mile 17 my calves had nearly run out of power. I walked a while. Was I resigned to walking in the last nine miles? I thought so, but along came Robert.

Robert was 26 years old, a worker in road construction from Monroe, Michigan. He, too, was tired from the hills, which even after the 15-mile mark continued 'til about mile 20.

After we had walked and shared thoughts for a while, Robert encouraged me to try to run again. On my second attempt the legs responded positively - slowly but with new life.

At this point more than one of the race officials' cars were asking if we wanted them to drive us to Peden Stadium. But Robert and I did not desire to be among the vanquished that day.

At this point, too, we knew there was only one runner behind us, and he had foot cramps, we were told. With four miles to go Robert looked back. "Hate to tell you this, Chuck, but that guy with the foot problem is about 70 yards back!"

With God's help I reached back for whatever was left and to Robert said, "Let's throw in a gradual build and see how badly he wants to catch us." After another half mile I asked Rob to look back briefly and to check on our running friend, whom, of course, we deeply admired for not giving up on this muggy April afternoon. Only after the race did we learn that 44 runners out of 146 starters did not finish. Rob said our friend was walking again.

We quickened our pace considerably as we entered the jogging path on the southeast corner of Ohio University, knowing that about 2.2 miles remained. My pace felt like a 7:30 now. I owed my renewed energy to Robert.

A half mile ahead I saw and passed a runner who had put away Robert and me earlier. By now Robert had surged ahead of me by 100 yards. An OU student doing her daily route came on to the path just after I had passed this latest runner. She, too, was a miracle. By running at a swift pace, she encouraged me to maintain mine. We ran side by side for a moment. I thanked her for helping me and edged ahead.

At this point the jogging path cuts a gentle curve like a sabre from southeast to northwest. Up ahead was another fellow runner walking, and we sailed on by. With less than a half mile to go I could see Peden Stadium and remembered the crisp autumn afternoons of days gone by when I as a college student had watched Coach Bob Hess' Bobcats chalk up many a victory. Up ahead Robert stopped momentarily to walk. I slowed a little to encourage him to run again. He resumed his gait, even quickened it a bit.

Just after I left the jogging path and approached the stadium, I saw familiar, loving faces – Martha and Robbie – and dear friends Bill, Wilma, and Billie Stacy, and Robert and I glided like skaters, soared like falcons across the 50 yards of grassy incline up to the south entrance of the stadium. We hit the all-weather track for 80 yards of dash to the finish line. Robert and I finished 98th and 99th respectively, and only three intrepid friends were to follow us across that line. Although Robert and I had slow times, we had finished the course.

Oh, by the way, I had forgotten to bring the Cold Duck – and the camera. I was really happy with the cups of cool water given by Wilma and Billie as I walked the cooldown with their support. Then five more cups of cola were all that I desired.

I will always savor this glorious day and may well try another marathon soon, but maybe a more level course on a cooler, less humid day. I wish to commend the winner, Allen Choma, of Columbus, Ohio, whose 2:33:06 under adverse conditions must be equivalent to a time way down near 2:10 or better. I recommend Athens as a challenging run.

Thoughts, personalities, and indelible memories

Not what we give but what we share
For the gift without the giver is bare.

James Russell Lowell

———◆◆◆◆———

Winners

Today, indeed, was special – and unusual in numerous ways. Here I was inside our home on a mild Sunday morning, watching TV. Ahh! You've guessed it! That's right – the New York City Marathon was featured at 10:30. I felt the exuberance and joy, the courage and purity of effort that I witnessed.

I marvelled at athletes in top form passing mile after mile at five-and-a-half, five, and even sub-five-minute paces. There were familiar faces of marathoners and distance runners present to run or to comment on the enormity of the runners' undertaking such a mission. Paul Pilkington, Bill Rodgers, and today's winner, Mexico's outstanding Andres Espinosa. I also salute Nadia Prasad's performance.

This runner would like very much to meet and lope a few miles with Uta Pippig (what a race!), Anne Marie Letko, Arturo Barrios (watch out in future competitions, folks!), and "double wow," a superb effort by the pride of Minnetonka, Minnesota – Bob Kempainen, today's runner-up.

I wish to add that there were more than 20,000 winners in today's race. You see, I have a poster bought several years ago that reveals this truth: "The race is not always to the swiftest / But to those who keep on running."

I respect every runner who keeps up his effort, whatever the pace. I applaud those who walk parts of the distance, too, while they summon the will and power to resume their running posture. Nowhere in my considerable years as an athlete have I seen more winners than in the venue of distance running.

Each runner has a story to tell, a story all his or her own. The more we learn, we discover the hero and heroine in ourselves and countless others. Running is good medicine, good sense, good fellowship. It puts us in touch with our bodies, our hearts, our place on earth. For many the lifestyle of running, when practiced moderately in balance with other facets of living, is a tonic helpful in keeping us in good health.

You probably know what happened as the telecast neared its end. Yup, I was out the door for a run. Today's romp once more delighted me. A bit humble at my eight-minute pace, I felt gratified with the 45-minute run and a mile cooldown back to home.

When you look into your mirror today or tomorrow, you're looking at the face of a winner – you! I am thankful for days I've toed the starting line, even days when I finished way back. Running fortifies us, making us gentle, patient, and resilient in a tough world.

The Winner and Still Champion

On June 18, 19, and 20, Ashland, Kentucky, enjoyed the company of running legend Bill Rodgers. Running enthusiasts of all ages were treated to a weekend of learning from Bill.

Bill's contributions began where I first caught up with him in hilly Wildwood Park. He had just completed a workout with 30 to 40 young runners ages 11 to 21. He titled his first session "How Not to Burn Out in Running." Some salient points were these: Read and learn everything you can about running; try to stay injury-free. He said that as a young runner he didn't run as far or as much as serious runners do today, and that was a blessing. Your shoes are important; they are critical. You can think and look for different strategies on how you can defeat your competition. And to the youngsters he stressed, "The best thing is that you're out here!"

Thursday evening we met in Our Lady of Bellfonte Hospital in a sports medicine facility equipped with everything. Their indoor track had lanes of the brightest colors. Why, I was feeling runner's high just being there. Bill called his remarks "Preparing for Competition." These are the points he highlighted: Take a look at the distance at which you really want to excel and focus on it. Say, "This is what I want to do, and I'm going to do it." We really need to take breaks from training and racing. Speed work is important. Learn how to train; some of it is trial and error. I like the feeling that I can always make a comeback. Get back to basics and do steady training. It's an emotional sport, and it's easy to get carried away. If you go out too fast and build up the lactic acid early in a long race, you're in serious trouble. Bill said that he's going to take some time off from running this year and wished everyone years of good running.

Friday morning the ol' adrenalin started pumping as I thought about the upcoming race. I knocked off a training run on some rolling terrain and hoped Saturday would dawn a bit cooler.

We enjoyed a pasta feast Friday evening sponsored by a local restaurant under a circus tent near the site of the race. Bill's next gems came later at the Town Center Mall. The topic: "Our Sport – Running." With care he expressed these ideas: Our sport is still a baby, a grassroots sport that people want to do on their own for their own feelings. The Olympics have defined our sport. Everything in running is in the head and the heart (spirit). People new to the sport feel they've found something special. Participation is the nitty gritty of running. And Bill referred to Dr. George Sheehan as he declared with praise, "We are all athletes!"

"What comes next?" you ask. Just what you'd expect. Saturday did dawn a bit cooler, and over 250 answered the call to the post for the 5K. Even nursing a strained back suffered in a Washington, D.C., workout on Wednesday, Bill built a commanding lead over a good field and breezed to victory in 15 and small change on a twisting course with a few hills.

Ashland and its capable Up-and-Running Club were the big winners that special weekend, for Bill Rodgers is the ultimate encourager of runners. The inimitable ambassador of enjoyable running summed up how running has helped him: "Running as a lifestyle has helped me improve my diet. I feel better physically and psychologically. I met my wife (Gail) while training. And running has been my business. I love to go places and see people get interested in running or walking to feel fit. It's a blast!"

If you are ever listening to Bill the day before a race, he'll probably sign off as he did in Ashland with these upbeat words: "I'll see you out there!" Likeable, thoughtful, gracious – the winner and still champion. "See you out there, Bill!"

Eyestone, Kilpatrick-Morris
Master America's 15-Miler

Do you like a fiercely-contested horse race? I mean neck and neck and elbow-to-elbow. If you do, then Charleston, West Virginia, on September 4 was the place to be. At the six-mile mark as they descended the South Side Bridge from grueling Loudon Heights, Ed Eyestone was literally the center man for what looked like a new dance step, flanked by Dan Held and Mark Curp.

Later on Held and Eyestone took command. With a mile and a half to go in the flat downtown section, Ed put on one of his patented moves to forge ahead. Winning at 1:14:52, he still didn't win in a cakewalk as Dan, having an excellent year and racing smooth as silk, closed hard, crossing the line at Laidley Field's cushioned track just 14 seconds back at 1:15:06.

Mark Curp, a three-time defending champion of this race, nailed down a solid third place in 1:16:54. Mark, along with Jon Sinclair, is one of the talented "elder statesmen" of road racing, having lifted running to new heights in long careers on the running scene. Both Mark and Jon have more great races in store, and being much more on the elderly side than they, I always root for them to do well. Both champions, they're always lots of fun to talk with, and gentlemen as well. When Mark signs anyone's race number, he follows his name with Isaiah 40:31, a beautiful passage about running and life.

Debbi Kilpatrick-Morris, the wiry speedster from Strongsville, Ohio, outlegged Jennifer Martin of Erie, Pennsylvania, in the stretch to capture her second Charleston win in a row with a herculean effort of 1:27:23, faster by 1:16 than last year's time and 19th overall out of 1,057 finishers.

Jennifer Martin, pounding strongly and in top form, was not far from Debbi, just 23 seconds back at 1:27:46. She remarked with a grin afterward, "Believe it or not, I do enjoy the hills." (In the early part of the course between miles two and six).

The pre-race pasta dinner and the post-race dinner both rated four stars in my book. The runners' clinic featured entertaining and informative tips and wisdom from Kitty Consolo, a splendid runner and storyteller, and Greg Meyer. Greg used to work and train with Bill Rodgers in Boston and still holds the world record for ten miles, I believe, set at one of my favorite races, the Cherry Blossom.

Charleston is a very good road race replete with large crowds of cheering spectators, urging on and encouraging the runners in the early uphill section. I personally dedicated my running of the race this year to a close friend of mine, a courageous man who experienced a severe stroke nearly five years ago. He and I played sports together for many a year. So it was a privilege for me to emblazon on chest and stomach in bold red, THIS ONE'S FOR YOU, and then his name.

Mitch Bentley Victorious
at 26th Athens Marathon

April 4th dawned crisp and sunny. At race time runners' spirits were buoyed by a 53-degree reading at the old courthouse. This hilly course, Ohio's oldest marathon, drew an adventurous field to battle the breezes which sometimes seem to blow in a runner's face both going out and coming back.

Ye olde writer opted for the half-marathon race in its third year. He knew the degree of difficulty of the longer trek from April of 1985, when in severe heat and humidity he finished his first marathon. Forty percent of the field that day did not.

Tom Stickel set a torrid pace in the half-marathon, and his stride flowed over hill and dale to set a new course record of 1:09:20. He was followed by Shannan Ritchie, John Foland, Tom Antle, and Stuart Calderwood.

On the other hand, Mitch Bentley had to earn his victory the hard way. I learned after the race that he had sustained knee problems in December and had to restrict his preparations for Athens to roughly three miles a day. But being defending champion, Mitch chose to endure considerable stress and pain. After breaking the tape, he collapsed onto the turf at Peden Stadium, home of Ohio University football and a beautiful site for the finish of this high-quality race. Someone wrapped blankets around his legs and gave him beverages and fruits as he felt better. Then Mitch was awarded the laurel wreath, specially flown in each year to the race from Athens, Greece, plus his trophy, indeed well deserved.

A little background on our champion. I first met him when he ran for Vinton County High School and I was coaching cross country for rival Warren Local. He blew away the competition and impressed me as a gentleman, too. He still does. He ran outstanding cross country for Ohio University and has consistently finished at or near the top in several highly competitive races in Ohio and West Virginia. At age 29 when his injury mends, Mitch will again be a threat to snare many a crown for years to come. As a teenager he built a mileage base that was second to none. He remains one of Ohio's best distance runners ever.

If you're looking for one of these two fine rural courses in a beautiful setting next April, consider Athens, Ohio. From a delicious spaghetti dinner to a spectacular stadium finish with your name called aloud as you hit the track for your sprint to the finish, it's an adventure worth taking.

Dos Santos Ignites
Parkersburg Half-Marathon

August 21 broke fairly cool. But lurking in the air – you guessed it – 80% humidity. It affected all of us (1,300 finishers), but Brazil's Delmir Dos Santos fought it off best of all. Delmir recovered from severe stomach cramps starting at mile five to outduel Kenya's Kip Kimeli, a bronze medalist at Barcelona, and Ed Eyestone to the tape. His time was 1:02:37, just 12 seconds off the course record set by Steve Kogo in 1989. On this humid monster of a day his performance at a pace of four minutes, 47 seconds per mile over a rolling course with numerous bumps and one serious hill was nothing short of incredible.

This race is a jewel, the third leg in the West Virginia Grand Prix Series where top runners battle it out for prize money. A runner must compete in and finish at least three of the races. Runners are also eligible for random prizes. The other races are the Cabell Huntington (Huntington, WV) Ten Miler, the Big Boy Distance Classic 20K, (Wheeling), and the Charleston Distance Run, (15 miles, Charleston). My pick of the litter is this one at Parkersburg.

What a field there was this year! Hold on to your hats, caps, or whatever. Leading the way in the top 23 were Dos Santos, Eyestone, Kimeli, Sammy Nyangincha, Paul Pilkington, Jeff Jacobs, Darrell General, Dan Held, Bo Reed, Don Janicki, Eddy Hellebuyck, Keith Dowling, Scott Bagley, Thomas O'Gara, David Mungai, Jeff Cannada, Doug Cronkite, Rick Sayre, Jon Sinclair, Mica Comstock, Paul Rimmerman, Mark Curp, and Doug Kurtis. Those guys' times ranged from 1:02:37 to 1:09:00.

After the race Eyestone praised the champion, who had out-toughed him despite adversity, with a spirited "You're an animal!" Dos Santos enjoyed a celebratory ride in a spiffy white convertible in the post-race parade, flanked by Eyestone and women's winner, Jennifer Martin, a rising star from Erie, Pennsylvania.

Martin paced herself to battle the humidity. She came up from fourth place to win the crown over Strongsville Ohio's Debbi Kilpatrick-Morris by 26 seconds. The women's field was billed as the strongest ever by Dorsey Cheuvront, race director.

Chris Fox Battles for Tape
at Huntington 10 Miler

April 17th emerged on the side of winter though the calendar read spring. With a race-time high of 40 degrees and winds of 15-20 miles an hour, the stage was set for a bone-chilling day.

Cabell Huntington Hospital again sponsored this distance classic, a scenic route through picturesque Huntington, West Virginia. The race is the first leg in the yearly Grand Prix championship of the state. The series includes the Big Boy 20K Classic in Wheeling, the Parkersburg Half-Marathon, and the Charleston 15 Miler.

The dash to the finish line at Riverfront Park was one to behold. Three weatherbeaten harriers nearly neck and neck, running against the stiff wind, sprinting all out toward the finish line. It was a bang-bang-a -bang picture as Hagerstown, Maryland's Chris Fox propelled his angular torso across in 48:13, just a tick ahead of Dan Held (Brown Deer, Wisconsin) in 48:14. Bingo! Then across came Tom O'Gara from Johnson City, Tennessee, in 48:16. Wow! What I would have given for a ringside seat. Instead I was back in the pack, battling the elements, not much enjoying the view from the bridge we crossed twice over the frigid Ohio.

The women's rush to the tape was also tight. Strongsville, Ohio's Debbi Kilpatrick kicked into a touch of overdrive to finish in 56:31, just a twinkle ahead of Tammy Slusser of Monroeville, Pennsylvania, who sped across in 56:59. In this writer's eyes Tammy's strength and speed just keep improving. It was a delight to share a food-filled table with her, and her husband Don (an outstanding runner himself) and Neji Marklouf who trains with Don Janicki in Colorado, running his first race in the USA. Neji hails from Tunisia.

Huntington's classic included a three-mile run. Setting the pace were winner Scott Liebimttn, 19, of Huntington, in 15:35 and runner-up Brett Perry, 18, in 15:46.

Chris Fox set the course record here in 1991. In this beautiful city with ultra-wide streets you might set a new 10-mile PR. With springtime weather you'll find the course fast and to your liking. I must admit, however, that it took three cups of gratis coffee with cream at Chi Chi's bar to defrost my achy, breaky face and jaw.

Just Thanks

Here it is, Wednesday evening, less than three days 'til the Parkersburg Half-Marathon. The training run went well today, but I cut it a mile short because the sun was bearing down. (I take two small capsules a day of a medicine, and the instructions remind me to be cautious of hot-weather activities). Tomorrow before the day becomes a scorcher, I think I'll do one more shorter run to round off for Saturday's race.

I just took a giant load of laundry off the clothesline and am building up courage to tackle our dirty dishes. Besides, I owe Martha a few treats. You should have seen that mountain of spaghetti, garlic bread, and salad she prepared for dinner. No carbohydrate deficiency here!

The beauty of running – ahhh! Some of my favorite recent memories on road or trail are these: wild yellow canaries, new-mown hay and its sweet perfume, sweetpeas in full blossom, bluebirds, apple trees just loaded, horses scurrying for cover (or are they really wanting to join me in racing the wind?) We could add butterflies (I marvel at their strength, range, and resilience), frogs, crickets, locusts, fireflies, the last scrumptious red raspberries to be picked after a run.

Now you kick back and think of your own list. I never cared much for some of British literature, but their penman John Keats had it right with his: "Beauty is Truth; Truth, Beauty. That is all ye know on earth and all ye need to know."

This year has not been gentle, but I think we're weathering the storms better now. I just give thanks for a girl named Martha, who has rescued this boy from the fates time and time again when most mortals would have ceased. And our son Rob, eighteen and a half. With all our clashes he and I are beginning to do so much better. We should, for the calendar's pages flip by so swiftly.

A cool breeze penetrates my chair under the spreading maple. A mosquito has just lost in its bid to drain my leg. Sometimes it feels special to sit and give thanks for health and all our gifts. We are blessed to be runners. In your next race I wish you joy.

Autumn Encores

If there were ever a time I savored a run more than this, I can't recall it. You see, a powerful flu virus knocked me flat on my backside five days ago and finally departed. I thought that the internal nuts and bolts were well enough recovered and that it was time today to put the rubber to the road.

Fortunately my diagnosis was on the money. After the first half-mile I felt like a well-lathered thoroughbred, breathing rhythmically, layered with rivulets of sweat and pacing in relaxed form. And what a day it was for December. The mercury was sliding from 47 to 50 as a noon church bell tolled its melody to all on a clear day. This, friends, is more our style, I thought, as fall pushed back winter into the shadows again.

At the turnaround point of my loop I was still running comfortably. The bright orange toboggan was keeping my head cozy but not hot, and the layers of shirts culminated in a thin windbreaker, supplemented by the ever-present bandanna to protect the lower throat.

My steps were straight and true. Today's pace was right for me. Slashing, arms pumping like a metronome, and gliding with the breeze, I reaffirmed my belief that I'll be out there running at least four days each week this winter. Why? 'Tis simple. Running strengthens me in body, mind, and spirit. Without its benefits and release, I am sometimes courting trouble.

Sunset caught up with this gem of a day. I visualized the race coming up in four days. I've done the preparation and now await the adventure on a course I've run just once before. One thing for sure, I plan to enjoy each step. And if all systems are go, I hope to come blazing across the finish line like Billy Mills in the 10,000 meters at the 1964 Olympics in Tokyo, completely spent and ready for the post-race dinner. I will have earned it.

Beyond Words

Today is a day beyond compare. It is a special day, my birthday, October fifteenth. It feels more like late spring than early autumn. We're no doubt in the 73-degree range, and I sit barechested in an idyllic backyard. My companion is Zukie, 40 pounds of black Labrador retriever-spaniel. He doesn't say much, but I figured if running with his larger dog Wily could help Jon Sinclair in his later years of road racing, a canine pal might help me hold onto whatever pace and speed I still possess.

Yesterday out on my northerly, rolling route I knocked nearly 30 seconds off the preceding try two days previous. I was happy with the improvement though it really wasn't a tempo run. With a 5K in two weeks I'll go for jaunts of five miles and 10K at various speeds to complement these "playing with speed" efforts. One week later is a five-miler, a hilly one, I'm told.

Next week is when my wife and I join hands with other race volunteers at the Columbus Marathon. We've been assigned captains' posts at the 24-mile water stop. I've completed a few marathons, but it will be equally satisfying to be helping this time.

What do I treasure today? Relatively good health, nothing too far out of kilter. A sweet and caring wife, who also earns "merit badges" by reminding me it's time to put in the old-fashioned (and a bit heavy) storm windows. (I'm happy to report that after one day on the project all are in but two).

The sweet gum and sugar maple trees in all their glory. The golden chrysanthemum I just planted out front. The gentle breeze, which kicks up rowdier once in a while, just to remind us that these halcyon days won't last forever. The son who just might go with us to the big homecoming football game tomorrow at Ohio University. My humble alma mater has lost 15 in a row, and I'm optimistic for a new beginning, a win. The granddaughters, Lauren and Megan, who recently gave me a heartwarming endurance test as they sat with me while I read book after book.

Then, too, there's our hobby-lifestyle-avocation, running. I'm grateful for every experience and challenge, every joy and new friend that running has brought my way. Many of the benefits have much carryover value in other areas of life. On this brilliantly dazzling, placid afternoon, I give thanks above and to my parents, who pointed me to sports as a noble pursuit. I'm going out to play now; I'm going running.

Balancing Competition, Enjoyment, and Volunteering

This gorgeous fall day catapulted me into action. What else can one do but share it with you. Today's sunrise was highlighted by 48 degrees of racing "cool." A race of 4.2 miles was on tap, and was I ever ready to drop down from the steady diet of 10, 12, 13, and 15 miles which had punctuated spring and summer. I wondered if recent workouts had generated enough production of leg speed, or would I think I was grinding out another long one?

Despite twinges of pain here and there, the race went well. I had invited a close friend Ralph Van Atta over to Parkersburg from Clarksburg. He and I finished within 15 seconds of each other, and we didn't rig it that way either. Within an hour after the Honey Festival Run, I gave my race shirt away to a young woman (Miranda), who shared that she had played clarinet in one of the bands that inspired us to keep battling Wheeling's hills in the Elby's Big Boy 20K Classic last May.

And that's the point of our thinking today, the need for balance between competitive running and serving the end of enjoyment of the activity itself. Two, three, or four times a year (I don't keep a count) a runner should wear the other shoe of a race volunteer worker or director. Where would we runners be without them? Seeing the races through new eyes rekindles flames of encouragement of beginning runners and passion for the simple beauty of our sport.

A runner also adds extra benefits by branching out into new distances and new destinations. These mini-vacations can sometimes coincide with family visits or other responsibilities. They can add sparkle to a marriage or friendship, and sometimes you just want to go to a new town on your own as an adventure.

I think often of the element of balance in running. For me running is a therapeutic force of much good if it is not overdone. Hope the fall is good for you. See you at the finish line, glistening with sweat, content, and thankful, for we are runners.

Treasure

The day before Christmas it is. Late this morning I churned the legs westward into a stiff winter wind. The first uphill was the roughest, and I was glad it was behind me. The rest of the route was rolling, like a children's roller coaster. I didn't set a torrid pace; it was effort enough to move rhythmically in the extra clothing, topped off like a fancy ice-cream sundae with purple, yellow, and red parka and white-brown woolen toboggan. Nevertheless, in my state of not feeling particularly fast or strong, I was happy being out there on the roads.

No other runners were on our little county road, but I had seen a mother and son out for a run in town earlier. Other runners inspire. On my jaunts replete with hard effort and bone-chilling cold, I became the adventurer once more. I witnessed the majesty of flocks of birds in rapid flight, locating food supplies and eating their fill. I reveled in the beauty of the undulating countryside as a thin coat of snow had adorned it for the season. My reverie was almost shattered when a large dog came bounding toward me from a house 250 feet away. Fortunately his owner was nearby and called the dog back just in time. The only other challenge was the semi-fogging of glasses, depending on wind direction. All in all, I was, as usual, a happy camper and gave oncoming motorists a friendly wave as most moved over a little out of courtesy.

Completing the workout, I felt a sense of peace. It is no secret that this hobby and lifestyle does much to sustain me in times of loss, disappointment, and stress. My heart is the heart of a runner; therefore, running is my treasure. I am honored and privileged to have been called to be a runner and to sing with gusto the melodious praises of running.

A Season of Anticipation

March came in like a lion three days ago. I found myself scraping ice off the windows and shoveling nearly a foot of slippery snow behind our car so that my wife and I could extricate ourselves from the motel parking lot in Washington, Pennsylvania. After some fairly taxing driving I was relieved to see marked improvement just west of Wheeling, West Virginia, as we entered Ohio.

As we feasted on Big Boy's epicurean breakfast-bar delights, I thought ahead to late May and the hilly 20 K scheduled for Wheeling, especially 29th Street hill. I have already registered for this one and look forward to the crowd's response to my Disney-inspired costume, which I will give away one piece at a time to young spectators along the course. It surely ranks as one of America's hardest, but I keep returning for many pleasant reasons.

I have recently sent away for entry forms for some longer races coming up soon. Signing up early forces me to train intelligently. I may not quite be ready for that first one but will use it as a slow training run for the second long race.

Anyway, back to the story. The timing of our breakfast made one in the afternoon perfect for my next training run. Since the day was warming into the low forties, I declined the sweat bottoms but wore shorts covered by thin racing pants, about three shirts and a jacket on top, and a bright orange cap from a race last fall.

The distance gently flew by, uphills and down and turnaround. I decided to shut down the "engines" at the bridge for the one-mile cooldown home. My right thumb stopped the chronometer at an unusual time – 34:56, a straight in card games. I interpreted this as a positive sign that a season of good training and racing lies ahead.

With this aura of hopeful excitement I'll move to a subject of utmost importance, running safety. A runner must realize that without respect for vigilance and drivers his health is in jeopardy. I insist on wearing highly visible running gear. I always stay on the left side of the road, and even when I'm well off the nearest lane, I give more ground to an approaching driver if he or she does not seem to be giving ground to me. When drivers do give ground as they approach, I give a friendly hands-up wave and a smiling "Thanks." That lets them know there's a considerate runner out there, sharing the road with them.

Probably the most dangerous aspect of running on a two-lane road is when one car passes another behind you. The best precaution is to look to your right each time you hear a vehicle behind you, for there occasionally is one passing another. I have had a few narrow escapes when I forgot to look, so now looking is automatic.

I also choose to run at times when the traffic is lighter. And certainly it makes no sense to run when slippery snow, heavy rain, or mud makes conditions conducive to losing one's footing on or near the road. If you ever elect to run on sidewalks through town, please don't worry about logging a fast time. It is imperative to slow way down, even to stop, and look and listen at every cross street, alley, business entrance, and intersection. I was almost a hood ornament once when a driver ran through a cross walk and barely stopped at a stop sign. I changed to a safer running route.

From my emphasis on safety I return to this glorious time of the year. Now is the time to look at some races you've never done and to make plans to give them a shot. How refreshing to explore and find a new training path! How much fun to find a new running friend and have some runs together, settling down for cold beverages and cordial conversation.

It is the time of year for rebirth and celebration. For what was once dormant is now springing back to life. Lace up your shoes, and put a smile on your face. We are the new Athenians, men and women, boys and girls, of Marathon. We are thankful for the capacity to enjoy the small wonders of life, the ones that really count. And we are grateful for running and every benefit that it makes possible. Just think. When warm weather returns (and it soon will), gardening, mowing, and yardwork will be outstanding workouts to strengthen our upper bodies for running!

See you at the finish line! (and the water stops along the way).

Many Thanks, "Doctor" Running

Going the extra mile was not easy today. This morning I set the goal of running a mile further than my longest run since I became ill in late December. It hit abruptly this time. Not super hard but super fast. I rushed to fill my prescription for what the doctor recommends for chemical imbalance in my head.

It's depression, and I've been battling it for nine straight years that I know of. In two of the nine winters I chose to be in a hospital because of the severity of the problems. Some treatments were not pleasant, but I'm thankful that they worked. I am no stranger to praying before going under anesthetic for help.

Even a week ago I didn't feel creative enough to write. My thinking was slow, and the passion to share my thoughts about running was missing. Today marks improvement. I've reached the turnaround and am more alert. Not until I reached that point could I rekindle the fire to write about my love for running.

I am certain that running regularly has sustained me through these episodes when body chemistry goes haywire. Experiences with training and racing have kept me from giving up, when that temptation is always there in the wings. It was with much effort that I suited up for winter's blasts to plod a 30 or 40-minute workout sometimes lap after lap in a church parking lot semi-dug-out from 28 inches of snow across the street from our home. One night it was mega-laps in the downstairs family room when snowdrifts and sub-zero temperatures rendered it too dangerous to be outdoors.

I'll be taking the energizing antidepressant medicine for a little while yet. I take a small dose of Lithium Carbonate, a lightweight metal salt, to keep the body chemistry in better balance year round. If you or any of your friends or relatives have experienced depression, it is indeed treatable. I am so grateful for doctors and medicines, my wife and family, and for running, which is excellent therapy as well as a joyful activity.

Different stresses can trigger an episode, and it is certainly an illness one does not choose to have. Aspects of it are powerful. Being a runner has helped me fight back from its clutches. At its worst it is more ferocious than "hitting the wall" in a long race.

In some people (myself included) depression accompanies Seasonal Affective Disorder, which is caused by the greatly diminished sunlight during the winter months. My wife and I recently went to a well-attended meeting at a Parkersburg, WV, hospital where a doctor explained the benefits of light treatments to simulate lengthening the hours of daylight.

Do not be ashamed to seek medical treatment and therapy for depression for yourself, a friend, or a relative. Read literature on the subject because understanding will help you to help yourself or someone else. Running continues to be important to my health. A muted sunshine was out there today with me on the roads, and was I ever soaking it in, grateful to be feeling better. The possibilities and enjoyments are returning, and I smile broadly as I recall vividly, "I really did go the extra mile today!"

Once more I am thankful that I am a runner. With reborn enthusiasm I wish for you strength of body, mind, and spirit. Cherish each new day, give thanks for everything, and have a wonderful run next time!

Resolutions Mom Would Like

In The New Year This Runner Resolves...

To put one foot after another

To leave more pizza and punch for later-finishing runners

To again dress in glorious costume for three or four races
to make abundantly clear that having fun is important

To wear suitable winter attire when training so that body
and soul survive January and February

To pray for a cool morning Memorial Day Saturday in Wheeling
for the Big Boy Classic 20K

To go to other races for the first time ever

To obey training and nutrition rules religiously, otherwise
I'll finish races after all the refreshments are gone!

To continue my practice of a mile or two jog-walk cooldown
after most training runs

To hydrate-hydrate-hydrate

To finish my eighth mile at the stadium when champion Mark Curp
is nearing the final approach at the Charleston 15 Miler

To lift high the joy of running wherever I go

To leave the first shoeprints in the new-fallen snow and to
marvel in the beauty of God's creation

To be more patient, kind, and forgiving

To keep on keeping on

To be kind and friendly to drivers but wary of dogs

To pick up beer and pop cans on cooldown walks

To talk to the animals – deer, birds, cows, woodchucks

To take my own pizza and punch to races, just in case. Ha!

Roadside Ramblings

Thanksgiving morning, 1987, the temperature was in the mid-40's and dawn was about to break. At 6:48 I left the motor inn near MacCorkle Avenue in my hometown, South Charleston, West Virginia, content to run just a four-mile workout as an injury, almost healed, was a bit tender.

Thanksgiving, and was I *thankful*! Just a year and a half ago I had emerged from the second of two trips to the hospital, finally whipping the arch-foe depression. Running helped me in that battle. I remember a calm sense of pride when the nurses in their nightly checks of blood pressure and pulse would find mine remarkably low and would say, "You have the pulse of a *runner*."

"Thank you; that's right; I am," I'd reply. A bit of running was even part of the therapy.

August, 1986, was another memorable date. I was hired to return to my work as a high school teacher, and my wife found work as a science and home economics instructor nearby. Martha deserves the Olympic gold medal for "marathon champion" in standing by her man in bad times as well as good. So with love and work on an even keel I am twice blessed.

Meanwhile back to the run. As I headed east, I rounded a turn, and there was a new Kroger's going up on the Ordnance Park baseball field where I played a little second base and batting practice pitcher for my high school Black Eagles. My fondest memory is hitting one out of the park one day with the wind gusting to left that afternoon. You see, I was not a power hitter. If I'd had an ounce of sense I'd have been out with the track or tennis team. But Dad had been a fantastic baseball and softball pitcher in his prime, and I didn't begin much running until age thirty-eight.

On I ran. The sun was starting its ascent. Yesterday had been glorious as Dad, my son Rob (age 13), and I had sliced away at golf balls over eighteen holes on a 72-degree day. I passed near the football field where the home team usually played *at* the sport. There were a few good seasons, but we were more known for our basketball prowess (AAA champs my senior year). My best memory there was on the track as Coach Tony Miller often had our phys. ed. class race once around the oval. I was almost always second as David Rollins was a shade faster at that distance.

At the Chevrolet dealer I turned right on E Street, passing familiar sights – a church, a corner within a stone's throw of my old junior high, my old high school, the movie theatre where many Saturday afternoons were spent with 3-D glasses, outer space flicks, cowboys, the Wizard of Oz, wow! Then I found myself on E again, having completed a bit of C and almost all of D. What an imaginative town, huh, with those street names?

Moving westward again, I saw the former Naval Ordnance Plant, largest one-story American war production facility in World War II, now idle after serving a stint as a German car company's stamping plant. I picked up the pace just a little, thinking about proper running form as usual. It wasn't long before the tall neon sign of the motor inn glared at me in the distance, towering above the I-64 bridge over the Kanawha River.

Here I was – a visitor again in my hometown. I gently beckoned to my wife and son to arise. A new day was dawning, and I had so much for which to be thankful.

It's two days later. Yesterday I knocked off the same run again (a bit faster) just to firmly etch those memories one more time into my being. Today I enjoyed a 10K training jaunt over hills, and my mind's on a young runner friend of mine with great desire, determination, and ability, competing in the Kinney High School National Cross Country Championship Regional in New York. And, of course, on my next race – Charlotte, January 2. Running in moderation continually brings a glow to my face and a warm smile and wave to many a passing motorist and *always* to a fellow brother or sister runner.

———————

Early to Rise

This Sunday morning in late May I am steeped in sunlight. It's 7 A.M. My lawn chair is securely planted in our driveway gravel, and I face the Marathon (gasoline) sign at the country store across the road. Around me are the working calls of cattle, roosters, woodpeckers, and doves. A robin runs his jagged 5K course in our yard, employing "sonar" to discover dinner under the turf. A few giant coal-carrying trucks make their runs today to keep the lights on and the engines of industry running. We've endured a long winter and a cool spring. All my garden seed has rotted in the ground. What to do? Just try, try again. We continually face the ebb and flow of win and loss, of challenge and change.

In road racing this year I've already battled Mother Nature's outpourings of rain, cold, and wind. Always there are elements of adventure and a common bond of brotherhood among all of us. I'm a little undertrained for the demanding 20K course this weekend at Wheeling but will aim myself toward that first long (two-mile) uphill and see what happens.

Last weekend's Revco-Cleveland Marathon and 10K contained a plethora of beauty and courage, of fun and camaraderie. I was privileged to see marathon winner Don Janicki successfully defend his title and come close to a course record, to chat with Janis Klecker and her husband Barney, and to visit with speedy master Doug Kurtis, who once again snared the master's crown. Tammy Slusser ran well and is likely to have some outstanding performances this year.

The day before the race Martha and I walked downtown a few blocks to see the new baseball park Jacobs Field (known also as Gateway Stadium). Ten minutes later a fellow with two extra tickets gave us one, and we took turns going in, witnessing a 9-3 Indians victory over Detroit.

With a delicious pizza and creamy-Italian-dressing salad on Saturday night and coffee and donuts before daybreak on raceday, I was well fortified to slosh through Cleveland's puddles and to battle the wind in our faces early in the race.

The warmth of almost-summer sun penetrates. It feels glorious compared to winter's chill. After hand-tilling and replanting the garden today, almost tasting the hoped-for cantaloupes and watermelons of August, I'll put on shorts and shoes for a short run.

So this morning, like most, it was "early to rise." I now gaze at the spectacular cherry blossoms and lilac-purple rhododendron flanked by irises and roses soon to bloom. The garden work beckons. This is our time to enjoy! And we don't often know whom we may be encouraging or inspiring by our presence or example. So keep up your running.

Maybe Ben Franklin was right when he wrote: "Early to bed, early to rise, Makes a man (or woman) healthy, wealthy, and wise." On this day I'm thankful to know the glow of good health. Though I'm still far behind the lead pack on wealth and wisdom, running helps to sustain me. When we're out there running, we're winners as long as we try

Glimpses of Truth

It's not unusual that there are a few irritants with which I'm trying to cope and "ride out to sea." I remember the spirit of Rudyard Kipling's memorable poem "If" where he urged, "If you can keep your head about you while others are losing theirs and blaming it on you . . . you'll be a man, my son." In this venture I know I'm not alone, for we are all frequently on the short end of disappointment, loss, pressures, and health problems.

In the midst of strife and conflict we can be so happy that we have running to remind us that we're still all right, good persons, and we can sometimes develop a whole new way of solving a problem or just letting go of it right there on the relaxing training run we're taking. Often an answer or a different, more healthful approach to a problem appears like "Aha!" after we've finished our play.

For several weeks I've prepared a bit for a longer race. But I'll be out there primarily to run at a steady pace and to listen to my body. I'm running because it's a friendly activity, and I meet wonderful people every place I run! A week ago I really enjoyed the annual picnic of our local running club (River City Runners, Parkersburg, WV), tossed a baseball with a teenager who could zip the ol' fastball, played with twin red-headed toddlers, finished a distant fourth in a sack race, and did pretty good damage to some delicious food.

In the half-marathon just two days away, I'll see beauty and truth all along the course. The elite runners will display power and grace. We'll all need stamina if the humidity soars. My favorite folks will be the water stop people. Maybe they'll have wet towels, too. And if and when I hear them say this runner's name with one block to go down Market Street to the finish line, you can bet I'll kick in a sprint for the Gipper.

Whether we're in the grueling last stages of a race or just out playing with speed and gliding at various paces, we capture our own glimpses of truth. We're out there. Life's not a spectator sport. Running patches up a nasty day, or an attitude turned sour. Running has integrity and forms part of the foundation for the way we live. With running come caring smiles and lots of laughter. Now that's good medicine, not to take ourselves too seriously in the scheme of things.

Well, race time is near. My reward tomorrow morning is a high-carbohydrate breakfast at a restaurant buffet. Remember, runners, we deserve treats like that. Try to keep a light element in some of your running, too, and its benefits to you will radiate and multiply for many years.

In a world of much that tends to wear on the human spirit, our running casts a huge net of satisfaction. It is partly passion and partly a calmness beyond measure. It is authentic; no one can take it away. It can refresh us like a simple cup of crystal-clear water. One could do worse than be a runner!

Meeting of the Shepherds

Here it is, the day before Labor Day and the day after my 11th running of the Charleston (WV) 15-Mile Distance Race. "Sore?" you ask. "Not bad, really." I just discreetly equalized the muscle tension between upper and lower body by mowing our long, deep ditch near the road out front. Feet are propped up on an Oriental garden in the yard. Sunning on a large rock in that garden are yesterday's running shoes. They whisper, "Put me on tomorrow for sure."

The story that follows is true. Perhaps something like it has happened to you, or it will someday. Perhaps, after reading it, you'll say, "No, that could never happen to me."

It all began on a sublime morning, yesterday, September 3rd. How often do you in mid-summer awaken to 55 degrees in southern West Virginia? Not very often.

The starter's gun sounded; we were off. Before our valiant band of over 1,000 runners knew it, we had crossed the incline of the first bridge and sped downriver to take a familiar left turn. The road is Oakwood Road, but racing lore has dubbed it "Capital Punishment Hill." It is aptly named. It is actually a series of hills, one long and steep, plus four smaller ones.

We then hit a major downhill and crossed back over the bridge into downtown Charleston. After a right turn we embarked on a long straightaway, then circled part of the beautiful grounds of the Capitol.

Despite the cool weather fatigue began to creep in steadily. Around mile ten we weaved our way through the main drag of the Sternwheel Regatta. I noticed several games of three-on-three basketball going on and remembered how a long run takes it out of my usually accurate 15 to 18 foot jump shot.

By mile 11 we had crossed another bridge and made a right turn onto Delaware Avenue. I looked to my right and saw a fellow obviously tired. He said he was ready to quit. I said, "I'm pretty tired myself. Tell you what. We'll run together. Slow and easy. Walk a bit when we want. That sound O.K.?"

"You bet it does!" John echoed, and onward we plodded. I selected a variety of targets to which we would run, some short and others challenging. John and I exchanged stories of recent events in our lives, and he continued to respond without complaint to our running system.

At the 14-mile mark there is each year a large pep band sponsored by the telephone company. As we passed, the last of the trumpet players and trombonists were packing away their gear, heading off to wherever today's teens go for a fast lunch. Were we dismayed? Never. "Just a mile left."

It was half a mile later when John told me how proud he would be to enter the stadium, for his wife and two young children were sitting in the stands, waiting patiently, hopefully. You see, in our sharing a few miles back John had told the amazing story of his recovery just three or four months ago from a serious brain ailment. This was his first run ever at the 15-mile distance.

Nearing the stadium, I kidded John as we saw a sign RUNNERS ONLY on the street by a string of orange cones. "Gotta run the rest of the way, no walking allowed." The all-weather track felt springy under my feet. After crossing the finish line I gave John a bear hug. He had earned it.

The rest of the post-race activities were enjoyable. But nothing was more satisfying than meeting John and blending my pace with his. I was his shepherd, and, you know, he was mine. He may have helped me far more than I assisted him. And how did we meet in that grueling part of yesterday's race? I think I know the answer.

———◆·◆·◆———

Short stories

I understand the large hearts of heroes,
The courage of present times and all times.

Walt Whitman

The End of the Road

What a glorious Saturday morning! Steve woke up early – six sharp – his usual rising time. He and his bride of 57 years, Christy, loved this little cottage. They had moved here 25 years ago, and Steve still picked huge harvests from his garden and fruit orchard.

He left Christy, still catching a few z's, and headed for the kitchen. He knew what he wanted. His favorite – buckwheat cakes! Twenty minutes later breakfast was on the table. He yelled down the hall, "Come and get it, honey. Breakfast is ready."

"O.K." She maneuvered out of bed a little more slowly than Steve. After all, they were 86. That ol' runnin' fool Steve was still running in road races up to 6.2 miles all over the eastern states. And Christy went along when she felt up to it. If she didn't, he went anyway. He'd take a friend along or just buddy up with another runner at the race. Besides, he was pretty well known in racing circles because he dressed up once or twice a year in outrageous costumes and wrote poetry shouting the praises of running.

After breakfast Christy came up beside Steve in their livingroom love seat as he was reading the morning paper over his second cup of coffee in his "CARPE DIEM" mug. "Hon," she said, "we're having a little company today."

"When?"

"About lunch time."

"Who? How many? You know I can't take large crowds – like Christmas shopping at some darned mall right after Thanksgiving."

"Aw, I think you'll like it, dear. It's something special."

And special it was. About 11:15 the cars and campers started meandering down the road from the blazing hills to the pristine lake. By noon traffic was backed up. Several hundred runners and former high school students – see, Steve had been an English teacher – had come to salute, to say thanks to him, to help him remember all the good times.

There was food. *My*, this was a *feast*! Barbecued ribs, corn on the cob, mouthwatering whole wheat rolls, and that sweet, lemony iced tea that Christy made in jugs, to wash it all down the tummy.

There were stories. Yeah, the one Ryan Walters told about the cross country team that ran off from Coach C. on a workout only to reappear minutes later after visiting some buddies nearby. Then Scott Woodburn reminded the crowd that he was the only one of Mr. C's students to ever enter the classroom once in awhile by sliding in on his keister. You'd have thought he was practicing to be a Ty Cobb or a Pete Rose. Nowadays he was a truck driver and a heckuva fine fellow.

After all the tributes had been paid and the belly laughs had echoed all over the lakefront, one of the guests said, "Steve, we want to hear from you. What do you have to say?"

"Well, I guess I feel about like Lou Gehrig as the moviemakers portrayed him in *Pride of the Yankees*." And as Steve said it over the microphone, it reverberated to the reunited friends and their families: "I consider myself, myself, myself, the luckiest man, man, man, on the face of the earth, earth, earth." Tears streamed down his face. "Thank you, boys. Thank you."

The coffees and teas were served as were huge slices of pie – cherry, coconut cream, chocolate, pumpkin, custard, blackberry. The folks said their goodbyes, and guests and families hugged the old coach and Christy and rambled up the road from which they had come.

That night Steve went to bed about ten. Just before he left Christy in the kitchen, he hugged her really tight and said, "Thanks, kid. How'd you ever keep it a secret? It was *great* – imagine – to see all the old gang again!" He gave her a kiss and said, "I'm turning in. I'm sleepy."

The next morning the sky again was blue. The sunlight sparkled and danced on the lake. Christy awakened at quarter 'til seven and went into the kitchen to start the oatmeal. Steve liked hot cereal in the late fall and all winter, too. He would probably jog five miles around the lake today since he had had no chance to do it yesterday.

Christy went into the bedroom and called, "Steve, time to get up." No answer. Again, "Steve, c'mon now. A little breakfast and then time to run." No answer.

She flipped on the lamp on the dresser near their bed. And then she saw. Steve would not run today. It was the end of the road. There was the hint of a smile on his face. Was he running in paradise already?!

A tribute to Dr.George Sheehan, a runner's runner

For thy sweet love rememb'red such wealth brings,
That then I scorn to change my state with kings.

William Shakespeare

Dream

Cold rain pelted hard against the bedroom windows. Ruth's calendar read December 3, but winter was coming on early. She looked with wonderment at the expanse of running trophies and awards on the wall and shelves across the pale blue carpet. Those days seemed so far away, but eight years had indeed gone by.

Then she had been at the top of the heap, NCAA champion, both cross country and in the 5k and 10k on the track. Her road racing acumen placed her consistently in the top five in the land. But then came a series of crushing blows.

The summer after Ruth Remarque had been graduated from Penn State, her mom and dad were killed when a semi skidded out of control into their car (the driver had been drinking heavily). So there she was in Carlisle, working as a veterinarian, sharing a practice. She still ran, but her heart wasn't truly in it.

About a year later she met a really decent man, Bill Jenkins. He understood well her needs, and she ran whenever she pleased but did not compete. They married in the spring and enjoyed the next five years. But one evening when Bill was over in Cleveland on business, Ruth's phone rang. "Mrs. Jenkins, this is Officer Stephen Kline of the Ohio Highway Patrol. I deeply regret to inform you that your husband was run over by a bank robber in a high-speed chase downtown at 4:30 P.M. He did not survive the massive injuries."

Fortunately for Ruth, relatives, friends, and clients of her business rallied round. Still she was numb and felt the enormity of the loss. She did something she had never before done to ease the pain. She drank, progressively more and more. Running even as a hobby ceased. It was all she could do to drag herself out of bed to go to her job.

Finally a friend, Rachel, realized just how deep Ruth was sinking. It was clear that she couldn't cope anymore. Gripped in the jaws of depression, Ruth saw a medical specialist. He advised an antidepressant (there was one available with no dangerous side-effects) and a return to her running. This would be part of her therapy as would sessions talking with her doctor.

It didn't take long. The depression lifted after about a month. The running felt surprisingly good. It energized her. Maybe, she thought, she could focus on goals and dreams again. The strength returned gradually to her muscles. She built up to nearly a full schedule at her work; she achieved a reasonable balance between working, exercising, and enjoying herself with a small circle of friends.

As Ruth sat engrossed in her Travis McGee mystery (halfway through with its protagonist hot on the trail of the bad guys), she thought, "Wonder if I could run competitively again?" Not hesitating long, she answered, "Why not train and see what happens!"

That was the beginning of change. Ruth's confidence grew as she orchestrated her training and masterfully mixed speed and distance, fartlek, tempos, and intervals. The Pennsylvania winter was gentler, and her frequent training made her a new person. Coming back from nearly the edge, she savored these moments where her body and mind dipped into total joy. Often a few of the top men runners in the state or down in Maryland called her and enjoyed long runs with her on Saturdays or Sundays. With them she held her own. They, too, encouraged her.

One of these runners (Steve), pleased at her level of speed and overall condition, asked one day, "Ruth, did you ever think about the New York City Marathon?"

"Well, maybe a little."

"Well, I think you should, maybe a lot ! You're ready to go for it all!"

Ruth knew he was right. She made a commitment to the dream. Following a careful plan, she entered a number of road races through spring and summer, winning several, finishing in the top five in all, and always learning something. Steve was competing and coaching her, too. She liked the way he treated her and felt comfortable by his side and content and happy wherever she was. He respected her as a runner, for she had built a sizeable mileage base filled with varied training sessions. And into her program she wisely integrated easy days and some swimming and biking. She planned to peak in New York.

September whisked by. Ruth was backing off from her heavy training regimen. She knew what the possibilities were and just hoped she could execute her plan to do her best. The women's field would be strong, including top runners from Kenya, Australia, South Africa, New Zealand, China, Russia, Mexico, Spain, and Portugal, among others, all well-trained.

In October Ruth and Steve went down into the mountains of western Maryland. He prescribed workouts in the range of 14 to 18 miles over old logging roads. Ruth felt an extra burst of stamina from these splendid runs. Eating popcorn and singing as Steve played guitar gave an atmosphere of holiday to this special getaway. Ruth revealed, "Steve, I do think I can run a good one, a sub–2:25."

"No doubt from this ol' country boy."

On the Friday of November's first week, two days before the big race, Steve and Ruth drove over to the "Big Apple." They relaxed in the hotel and watched "Forrest Gump" and "The Princess Bride" on VCR, two of her favorite movies. A good friend of Steve's from the NYRRC drove them around the course early on Saturday morning. Now Ruth felt totally prepared.

Raceday dawned at an invigorating 36 degrees with virtually no wind. Ruth had slept well, and when Steve knocked on the door, she answered with a smile, "Good morning, coach. Maybe this is the day!"

"Could be, runner. You're in charge out there. Remember that."

So, enjoying some hot coffee with whole wheat toast and jam (she had baked the bread herself), she went about her usual ritual of visualizing what might transpire on the rambling course.

Ruth arrived at the starting area 50 minutes early. She began the gentle warmup that was all her own. Steve jogged with her for awhile, then wished her his best and left to head out to his designed spot on the course. To him Ruth cheerfully sang out, "You know, everything feels good today."

As Steve kissed her goodbye, he smiled broadly and proclaimed, "You've been waiting for this for a long time. Go get 'em, tiger!"

At 15 minutes until the start Ruth was ushered into her spot on row one. Assembled around her were other powerful distance women. Ruth politely said hi to those nearby. She was deep in reverie as the national anthem's strains enveloped the mass of runners. An invocation asked resolutely for all runners to finish the course safely. And then – bang! – they were off.

From Staten Island, crossing the Verrazano-Narrows Bridge, Ruth comfortably became one with the leaders, numbering 16, spread out over two loose groups, close together. In this elite pack with a few more sprinkled behind 30 to 50 yards were champions of many nations – Russia, China, Spain, Italy, Portugal, Kenya, Japan, Mexico, New Zealand, Australia, Brazil, South Africa, and USA. From how it looked at the start, this was anybody's race.

The leader's split at mile one was 5:30. Ruth felt fine with that, strong even. They glided into Brooklyn off the bridge and chewed up Fourth Avenue. At 10k the pack remained quite intact, the pace steady.

Between mile nine and ten the leading threesome upped the tempo to 5:15 and forged ahead. Not wanting to be way back at this stage, Ruth postured herself near the vanguard of the pack chasing the speedy trio. On Manhattan Avenue just past mile 12 the faster pace proved to be too much for about half of the number, who dropped back considerably. Ruth ran in eighth position, not far from Russian ace Petrova, who, in fourth, led this group of five. The frontrunners, holding on firmly, included Xi Huan, China's best, Kinjala of Kenya, and Martin of New Zealand, coached by master's legend John Campbell. Just ahead of Ruth lay Espinosa of Mexico, Lopes of Portugal, and Ando of Japan.

The torrent of runners crossed the Pulaski Bridge into Queens. Again the pace eased to 5:35. Ruth could see it was to be a tactical battle. She would have to select carefully her times and places to make the right moves. Queens flew by. Ruth's thoughts drifted to Steve and how wonderful he had been to her through the hard times and how he had trained her with ever so much care and expertise.

She was floating, strong, under control. Nearly beside her were Americans Joan Benoit Samuelson and Anne Marie Letko. What an honor to be running with them!

Entering Manhattan from the 59th Street Bridge, Ruth looked to her left and saw Joan accelerate on a downhill, one with plenty of promise. On the right Anne went by, too. Ruth accompanied them, and like three gazelles, they caught and buried the three ahead of them. Running in tandem, they were poetry in motion. As First Avenue passed 115th Street and the leaders crossed the Willis Avenue Bridge, Ruth, Joan, and Anne were closing the gap.

Breezing along Fifth Avenue, still steady and in unison, the three caught Martin and left her 200 yards back. Then Kinjala succumbed to a muscle pull and dropped back and out of contention. But speeding down Fifth Avenue at 120th Street, Anne felt the tug of an old leg injury and eased off, giving Ruth and Joan an 80-yard lead over her. They looked ahead 80 more yards to Huan, still pounding like a metronome with a Diehard battery.

Trouble struck when least expected as Ruth and Joan chased Xi Huan into Central Park. A novice waterstop volunteer came out with two cups and lost her footing, striking her squarely, sending her onto the pavement. Stunned and shaken, Ruth suddenly felt someone pulling her to her feet. It was Joan! A very quick "thanks a lot" and two genuine smiles later, both were on their way again. Anne had passed them during the fall, but in the next quarter mile they moved by her with new fervor. A little scratched on both palms and banged up on her left knee, but none the worse for wear, Ruth felt the strength of her youth return once more.

When Ruth, with Joan in tow, reached the 24-mile mark, to her left she saw Steve's neon yellow parka. His call to her was undeniably clear: "Turn it on now, Ruth. A hundred yards and close hard; get 'em!" Activated and swelled with his love and her pride as a runner, she began a build that moved her past Joan. Her sights she set on China's best, Xi Huan.

"Get up there, form, form; use your head!" Ruth articulated to herself as she narrowed the gap. Deep in Central Park now where 66th intersects East Drive on the course, she was just 30 yards back. Sticking there the next half mile, she detected a measure of fatigue in Xi's arm carriage and posture.

"Time to do it!" and Ruth put the hammer down enough to open a 40-yard lead. There was no "wall" this time; nothing had stopped her, not even the spill. It was time to build on the lead, to control rhythm and form, and to remember all the tips – mental, physical, and spiritual – which she and Steve had shared and learned together.

Ruth moved onto West Drive and heard the deafening noise of the crowd, packed on both sides of the course. She took a quick look back and saw two runners beginning to close the gap. Yikes! Summoning one more burst of power, Ruth reached back for a gradual build through all her gears, culminating in a sprint, reminding her of her finishing kick on the track at Penn State. Up ahead she spied the mammoth finish line and drove relentlessly through the tape – snap! At that instant the chronomix overhead flashed 2:24:49.

Exhaustion. Sheer, happy exhaustion. Five seconds later Ruth turned for an instant. Boom, bah boom! Joan burst through into the chute, just a second and a half ahead of Xi Huan. Joan had indeed turned on a super close, reaffirming her world-class abilities and reigniting fans' memories of her '88 Olympics victory.

Warm blanket 'round her, Ruth basked in the radiance that only victory can bring. It seemed like an eternity but was only a few minutes 'til Steve met her in an enclosed area.

"You did it, Ruth; you did all we dreamed of and more!"

Flushed with tears of joy, Ruth gave Steve a mighty hug of deep friendship. "Steve, my wildest dream came true out there today."

"I know, and in that you can take much pride. What a dream!"

Ruth was on angels' wings as the awards ceremony progressed. She looked upon the sculpture of Fred Lebow nearby and felt his strength and courage course through her body. She radiated all the qualities of a champion.

First and Last

The news hit hard, I faced the blow
A hero flown away
Oh, George, oh, Doctor Sheehan, sir
Your star still beams its ray.

When this old world turns grimy gray
And days are laced with pain
I'll think of you, your winning way
And join the race again.

For you discovered secrets
That mortals seldom do
And in the halls of running folk
You *are* the proud, the few.

Yes, you have been our captain
Crossed finish line, race won
Engender in our hearts and minds
To play and have much fun.

I place the victor's laurel wreath
O'er noble head and brow
And just say, "Thanks for everything!"
Once more renew my vow.

To be all that I can be
To light the eternal flame
Respecting purity of heart
I'll honor well thy name.

May I so live to spread the word
That running's right for all
Keeps body–soul in harmony
Builds strength to crest the wall.

I pledge to keep on running
From now until the last
And proudly wave the banner
'Til my time, too, is past.

—•◦•◦•—

The victory lap

Genius is one per cent inspiration
and ninety-nine per cent perspiration.

Thomas A. Edison

Sailing

April 28th, the humidity's rising, one of those azure days
  To tread with the sun bearing down
Baking me lightly into cinnamon, like a compact spud
  Better begin promptly, three hours past breakfast.

Ah! Wind's out of the north-northeast
  A breeze of substance and in my face
It will slow me down and cool me, too
  I win both ways, plus it'll push me home.

Not exactly flying today, but smooth am I
  Rhythmic exhalations and loose armswings
Propel me toward the goal
  Relax me on my way.

It's a perfect recipe, this running and me
  This sweat profusely pouring cleanses much
A purring engine, I vault hills up and down
  Being me and sailing away.

Ballad for All Time

What I'd like to do?
The impossible, of course
Slow down the hands of time
And let happy hours just drip ever so slowly.

I'd catch all these races in my bottle
All the fun-loving folks on a perpetual videotape
And relive and expand all the good times
We started.

A collage I'd construct of every favorite run
And play it over again when I needed a jolt
Each lake and soaring eagle would occupy a
Prime piece of my mental landscape.

Of course, we miss the mark in this dream
But we can come close
And squeeze each day for all it's worth
Taking jubilation to a new dimension.

So gather round me now
And roll our camaraderie up into one ball
And change us from coachmen to running mice
To feast at the cheese of life.

Ditches Have Feelings, Too

I'm the ditch beside the road
    Where you take your training run
I see it all from ringside seat
    While you sweat and have your fun.

I watch the flying dervishes, the cars and trucks so fast
    Just rushing to and fro, oh my, my time for peace has passed
And what they gain from speeding so, I really have no clue
    The best part of my day is when it's time to be with you.

You gently float as you go by, a smile upon your face
    No singleminded lust for speed, that's surely no disgrace
My forest creatures needn't fear that you will crush their day
    As you're a turtle-hare yourself, just living, come what may.

So you, you happy wanderer, run long your chosen route
    For 'bout this ratrace speeding by, I give not e'en a toot
Refresh the wayward human race, continue what you do
    I'll dress in hues of brightest green to mark the way for you.

Rhythm and Rhyme

Orange shorts, brown hair
    This day, so fair
Breeze blows, just right
    Warmed up, not tight.

Cars yield, I wave
    Friends, kids, toot, rave
Special I feel
    Not a big deal.

Decide short run
    Mostly for fun
Turn'round comes quick
    Legs loose, arms click.

Slow pace takes road
    Gives me light load
We need these times
    Refresh like limes.

Finished, iced tea
    Grand romp was free
Morning will break
    Long run I'll take.

Whate'er the world
    Dishes my way
This path's the best
    "Hip, hip hooray!"

Summer Evening

Glowing sunset, fiery orb
　　Let me now some truth absorb
Ball in heaven, falling fast
　　Help me catch a spark that lasts.

I'd been seeking far and wide
　　For a life that satisfied
Realized it's all around
　　Embraces us without a sound.

The arrow's sent from up above
　　It's bathed in faith and steeped in love
Full of hope, it enters in
　　And with its strength our race we win.

Tonight the sky puts on a show
　　I know the storm will follow though
Low clouds zoom in from the southwest
　　And thunder soon will be our guest.

Such storms are like a running race
　　They temper us and slow our pace
Repairing body, mind, and soul
　　They cool our jets, help make us whole.

Mellow colors cover sky, and gray infuses all
　　But knowing that the storm will pass, I'll not refuse the call
Of open road tomorrow, old shoes, old socks, new me!
　　The scenery changes always; but sure, the best is free.

Welcome to My Road

Glad you came over, said yes to the call
    Go stride for stride with me, say, this is a ball!
I know this route backwards and forwards it seems
    And stuff that I see here is filled with best dreams.

These are the spots where wild sweetpeas all grow
    And this babbling brook makes cool melodies flow
Muddy ruts and cracked asphalt at road's weary edge
    Dictate attention or an ankle might wedge.

That little toy soldier lying straight up ahead
    Will not see his master, whose dad sped, it's said
Oh, you'll see bright canaries as they dart on close by
    And we could 'bout join 'em if we only could fly.

But here we are earthward, the right spot for love
    Just run any path, why, it fits like a glove
The secret's we're out here and dancing with joy
    May our roads ramble gently – woman, man, girl, or boy.

November Green

Looking out my open window
    Saw a squirrel sprint swiftly by
What a fall! The best one ever
    Grass still green, amazed am I.

Run I will a long one, singing
    Buoyant, out there in my shoes
Soon will cold and dark days follow
    Not one second left to lose.

Hour 'til lunch, then three hours later
    I'll be out there in my prime
Uphills, down, and sculptured pathways
    Always something new to climb.

Thinking now of races future
    Increase planning, plot them well
Run your heart out for the glory
    There'll be stories fit to tell.

May this green day live forever
    Etch a memory on my soul
Carry me through rain and shadow
    Bless me please and keep me whole.

The Perennial Question

Memory, and the mind turns backward
Touching, feeling, and hearing yesterdays beyond compare
Seeing friends and foes alike
Reliving the hugs, kisses, soft words, angry words
Searching for a clear message
That I am a good person
Accept me as I am, I'm really trying
To figure out how I fit in.

But enough of that, time to reverse engines
And after brief reflection go full throttle ahead
I march to my own drummer
And eagerly view the sunrise
Of a day which soon will whisk by
My time to act is now.

So

"So you're that writer, did you run today
Did it make you happy, was it mostly play
Were you dressed all right, did your face just beam
Was the sun your guide, did you ford a stream?"

"Yep, I ran for me, and the joy soaked through
Though 'twas late December, why, the sky was blue
Had a smile so wide, could have jumped the moon
Every sinew pulsed, 'AOK', in tune."

"Are you right aware, pilgrim son, good lad
That this sport affirms and guards you from bad
It puts you in wonder of the earth around
As you stride, caretaker, on this hallowed ground."

"It took a while, Dad, 'fore it dawned on me
That this way of life was both dear and free
I can glide like cheetah, I can laugh out loud
I can love more freely, of this I'm most proud."

"Oh, my boy so precious, let me now make clear
That this world turns quickly – minute, day, month, year
May you train with wisdom, may your friends increase
And your life be balanced, and your deeds not cease."

"Dear most noble father, you do guide me well
And with thanks aplenty, I your tale will tell
If our motto's striving, finishing, our goal
There'll be no regretting, for our lives are whole."

Marching

Rev up your purring bodies
    And your best colors don
Spring out of bed at daybreak
    For time goes marching on.

The runs that once were summer
    Are now the fall for sure
And winds that blow will bring the snow
    All cold and rough, but pure.

These days I start a thinkin'
    How richly I am blessed
To hit the trail where'er I please
    North, south, or east or west.

The monumental lessons
    I learn as I go by
Digest and use, light well my fuse
    Give me the strength to try.

To win the inner battles
    When lesser men would quit
Though in great pain I rise again
    To love and give; that's it!

They say the longest journey
    Begins with single step
So join the throng and come along
    Add to the world some pep!

Your Lake

Winding down after running long
    I started 'cross the bridge
You heard my alien steps
    And quickly put a few hundred yards
Between us.

Once more feelings surged in my heart
    In awe of your graceful arcs
Your pounding wings, making effortless
    The swaths you cut in all weather
Through sky.

I think of your strength and courage
    Now in late November
When savage winds and deep, freezing snows
    Will again test your mettle
Your will.

O great blue heron, I lift a prayer to you
    To make it through the storms of winter
Return 'mid vernal breezes
    Again my comrade be, as this runner
Views your majesty
    This is your lake, I merely pass by.

———•◦•———

Miracles

Slowly head drops, eyelids weary
    Body seeks rest on comfy couch
The runner thinks hard on just what image
    Defines this day.

Aha! He remembers it well
    With about 2.8 miles left in the race
He looked all around and found
    A most dazzling mixture.

Of fleet-footed youngsters skirting on ahead
    (Oh, how they would've made fine employees of *Oliver*'s Fagin!)
And girls, women, men, masters, grand, serious – a rainbow
    Of every size, shape, mind, and soul in the universe.

All, out there, yes, out there!
    With every step brightening the way
For all of us
    As we headed toward our goal.

A darn sight better than watching the "tube"
    These folks were revealing their inner core
As seekers of Truth, and honest ones at that
    Enjoying one another, the pace and the chase.

Remember it well, all ye who lace the shoes and don the shorts
    You are part of a vast sea of miracles
And by unlocking doors with your smile and effort
    You might be passing on these miracles to others.